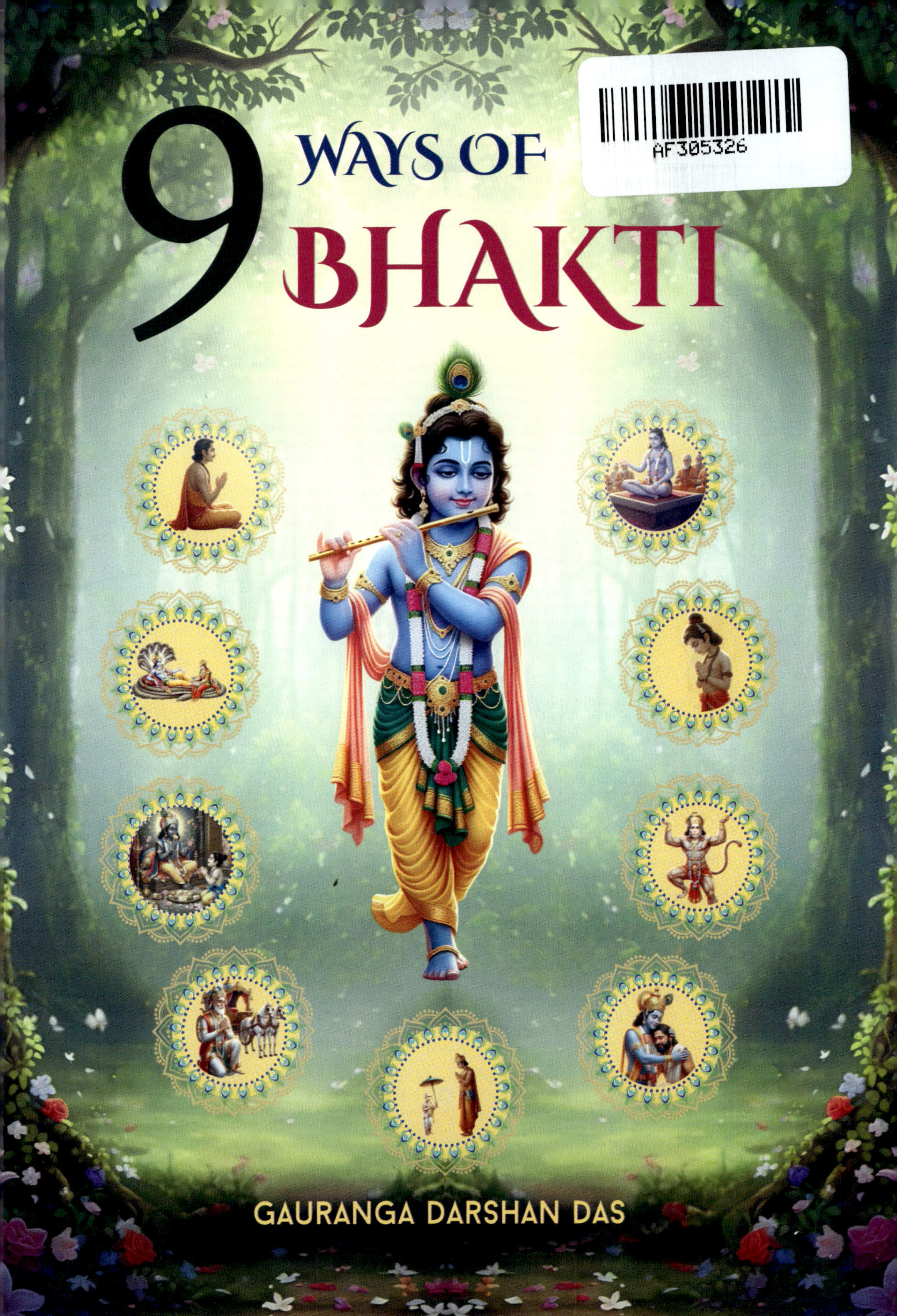


9 WAYS OF
BHAKTI
GAURANGA DARSHAN DAS

Bhaktivedanta Vidyapitha

ISKCON Govardhan Ecovillage, Galtare, Hamrapur Post,

Wada Taluka, Palghar District, Maharashtra, India – 421303

www.vidyapitha.in

Published and Printed by

Tulsi Books (A division of Sri Tulsi Trust),

7. K. M. Munshi marg, Girgaum Chowpatty,

Mumbai, India – 400007.

www.tulsibooks.com | tulsibookssales@gmail.com



Visit gaurangadarshan.com for all the books, articles, videos, audios, courses, sloka recitations and other spiritual & educational resources from the author.

**9 WAYS OF BHAKTI**
ISBN: 978-81-989997-3-3
First Printing – September 2025: 2,000 Copies

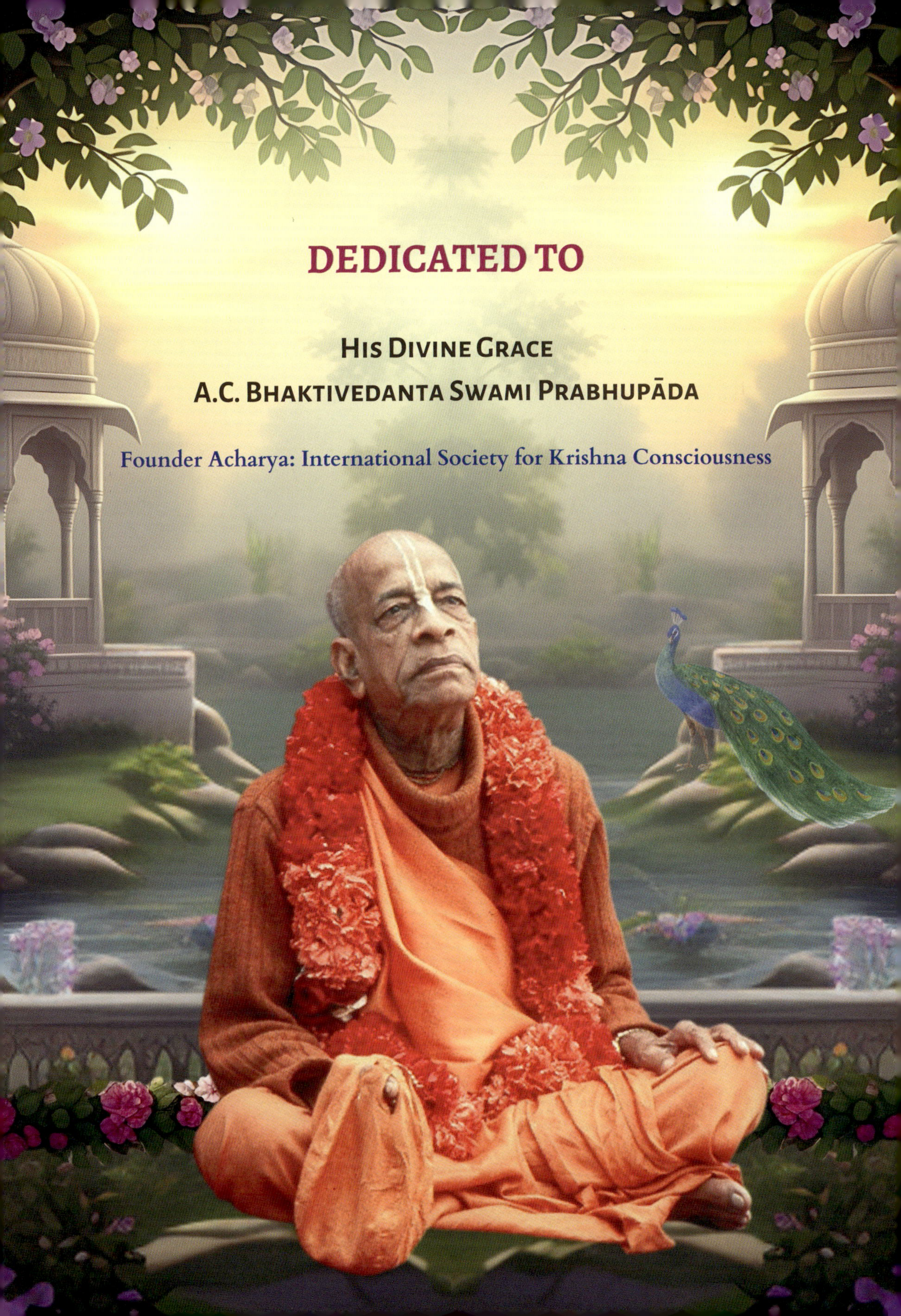

DEDICATED TO

His Divine Grace
A.C. Bhaktivedanta Swami Prabhupāda

Founder Acharya: International Society for Krishna Consciousness

# Contents

1
Śravaṇam
2
Kīrtanam
3
Smaraṇam
4
Pāda-sevanam
5
Arcanam
6
Vandanam
7
Dāsyaṁ
8
Sakhyam
9
Ātma-Nivedanam
9
WAYS OF
BHAKTI

# PREFACE

Childhood is the best time to start practicing *bhakti*. Children are naturally pure-hearted, impressionable, full of energy, enthusiasm, and curiosity. A tender plant grows straight and strong when cared for properly. In the same way, a child's heart becomes deeply rooted in devotion when nourished with the teachings and practices of *bhakti* from the beginning.

In the *Śrīmad-Bhāgavatam*, five-year-old Prahlāda, one of the greatest devotees of Lord Viṣṇu, gives this special instruction:

*kaumāra ācaret prājño dharmān bhāgavatān iha*
*durlabhaṁ mānuṣaṁ janma tad apy adhruvam arthadam*

"From early childhood, a wise person should practice devotional service. Human life is very rare. Although temporary, it is of great value, because it allows one to practice bhakti and attain the Lord." (SB 7.6.1)

The scriptures house abundant inspiring examples of children who practiced *bhakti* — Dhruva, Prahlāda, Parīkṣit, Uddhava, and many others. Prahlāda Mahārāja also brought to light the nine powerful ways of bhakti, namely:

*śravaṇaṁ kīrtanaṁ viṣṇoḥ smaraṇaṁ pāda-sevanam*
*arcanaṁ vandanaṁ dāsyaṁ sakhyam ātma-nivedanam*

"Hearing about Lord Viṣṇu, chanting His glories, remembering Him, serving His lotus feet, worshiping Him, offering prayers, serving Him as a servant, becoming His friend, and surrendering everything to Him — these nine are the processes of devotional service." (SB 7.5.23)

These nine ways are like nine jewels, each radiant with its own beauty, each one bringing us closer to Lord Kṛṣṇa.

*9 Ways of Bhakti* is my humble attempt to assist children to discover how joyful and natural it is to perform devotional service unto Kṛṣṇa. Each chapter explains one of the nine processes in simple language, with stories from the *Śrīmad-Bhāgavatam, Bhagavad-gītā, Rāmāyaṇa, Caitanya-caritāmṛta,* and the lives of saints. Selected *ślokas,* along with practical takeaways and activities ensure consistent interactiveness. To top that, resplendent illustrations bring the stories alive.

The purpose of this book is not only to deliver information but to help children feel a deep, personal connection with Kṛṣṇa — to see Him as their closest friend, protector, and guide.

The landscape of the world today is loaded with distractions. But when children learn to perform one or more or all the 9 processes of bhakti, they will experience their hearts fill up with peace, joy, and strength. The very essence of this book is that children arrive at the realization that the Lord is always with them — at school, at home, on the playground, and everywhere.

Just as Prahlāda Mahārāja told his classmates, "My dear friends, don't wait until you are old. Begin *bhakti* now, in childhood!" — this book is meant to help today's children begin their own journey of devotion.

My prayer is that every child who reads this book discovers one or more of these nine ways as their own secret doorway to grow closer to Lord Kṛṣṇa — step by step... and maybe even in a joyful sprint!

With heartfelt wishes and lots of love,
Gauranga Darshan Das

# 1

# ŚRAVAṆAM

## Hearing

*Hearing about Kṛṣṇa waters the seed of love in our hearts.*

*Śravaṇam* means hearing the topics of the Supreme Lord Kṛṣṇa — His sweet names, His beautiful forms, His divine qualities, and His wonderful adventures. It is the very first step in the journey of *bhakti* and the foundation on which all other devotional practices stand.

When we hear about Kṛṣṇa from loving devotees who speak based on authorized scriptures, our hearts become filled with devotion and joy. Hearing acts like watering a little seed of love for Kṛṣṇa that is already present within our hearts. With regular watering, that seed grows into a blossoming plant with flowers of devotion and fruits of love.

All of us are eternal children of the Supreme Father, Kṛṣṇa, but many people are unaware of, or have forgotten, their relationship with Him. Through the process of *Śravaṇam*, we are reminded of that bond and inspired to revive it by worshiping and serving Him.

*śṛṇvataḥ śraddhayā nityaṁ  gṛṇataś ca sva-ceṣṭitam*
*kālena nāti dīrgheṇa  bhagavān vaśate hṛdi*

"The Lord quickly manifests in the heart of a devotee who continually hears about Him, with faith and serious endeavour." (SB 2.8.4)

Topics related to Kṛṣṇa are called *Kṛṣṇa-kathā,* and they are of two types:

## TWO TYPES OF KṚṢṆA-KATHĀ

### 1 TOPICS SPOKEN BY KṚṢṆA

*Bhagavad-gītā,* which teaches us important truths and philosophy of life.

### 2 TOPICS SPOKEN ABOUT KṚṢṆA

*Śrīmad-Bhāgavatam,* which describes the amazing stories of Kṛṣṇa and His devotees.

Both books are treasures that guide us towards the eternal shelter of Lord Kṛṣṇa. Apart from these two, there are many other wonderful *Vaiṣṇava* scriptures, and hearing them makes us firm in our devotion to Kṛṣṇa.

The scriptures teach us both philosophy and pastimes of the Lord, hearing which benefits us in the following ways:

Hearing philosophy sharpens our intelligence, dispels our doubts, and brings us from confusion to clarity.

Hearing pastimes of the Lord enlivens our minds, and infuses our hearts with love for Him.

As the *Śrīmad-Bhāgavatam* (1.7.7) says:

*yasyāṁ vai śrūyamāṇāyāṁ kṛṣṇe parama-pūruṣe*
*bhaktir utpadyate puṁsaḥ śoka-moha-bhayāpahā*

"When we hear about Kṛṣṇa, the Supreme Person, love for Him awakens in our heart, and sorrow, fear, and confusion go away."

Our ears are like the doors to the home of our heart. When we hear *Kṛṣṇa-kathā* with open ears, Kṛṣṇa Himself walks in and makes our heart His home forever! Are you ready to invite Kṛṣṇa into your heart and keep Him there always? Then don't wait — start hearing His stories every day!

Here are some wonderful examples of devotees whose lives were transformed by hearing from the Lord or hearing about the Lord.

### DID YOU KNOW?

*Śravaṇam* is not only about hearing the Lord's glories but also about hearing the lives of His pure-hearted devotees. Their examples inspire us to follow in their footsteps and develop deep devotion to Kṛṣṇa.

# 1. Princess Rukmiṇī Marries Kṛṣṇa

In the kingdom of Vidarbha lived Princess Rukmiṇī, famous for her beauty, wisdom, and gentle nature. Many saintly devotees like Nārada Muni, visited her palace and spoke to her about Lord Kṛṣṇa's courage, kindness and virtues.

Rukmiṇī would listen attentively. Each word about Kṛṣṇa was like a jewel being placed in her heart. She had never seen Him, yet just by hearing about Him, she developed deep affection. She made up her mind: "I will marry only Kṛṣṇa."
But her brother Rukmī disliked Kṛṣṇa and wanted her to marry his friend Śiśupāla. Rukmiṇī was distressed, but she wrote a heartfelt letter to Kṛṣṇa and sent it secretly through a *brāhmaṇa*. On the day of her wedding, Kṛṣṇa arrived in a golden chariot, defeated all the opponents, and carried Rukmiṇī to Dvārakā and married her.
Another princess named Nāgnajitī also fell in love with Kṛṣṇa by heairng about Him from Nārada Muni.

*Śravaṇam fills the heart with a longing to attain Kṛṣṇa.*

# 2. Arjuna Fights With Wisdom

Before the great battle of *Kurukṣetra,* Arjuna stood on his chariot, looking at the two armies. He saw his teachers, cousins, and friends on both sides, ready to fight. His hands trembled, his bow slipped, and his mind became filled with doubt.
"I don't want to fight," he told Lord Kṛṣṇa, his charioteer.

To inspire him Kṛṣṇa spoke the *Bhagavad-gītā* — explaining the science of soul, duty, devotion, and surrender. Arjuna heard carefully. His doubts melted away. His heart became strong. With full clarity and conviction, knowing what was right, Arjuna fought with courage alongside his brothers, the Pāṇḍavas, and defeated the army of the wicked Duryodhana.

*Hearing Bhagavad-gītā removes doubts and motivates us to perform our duty against all odds.*

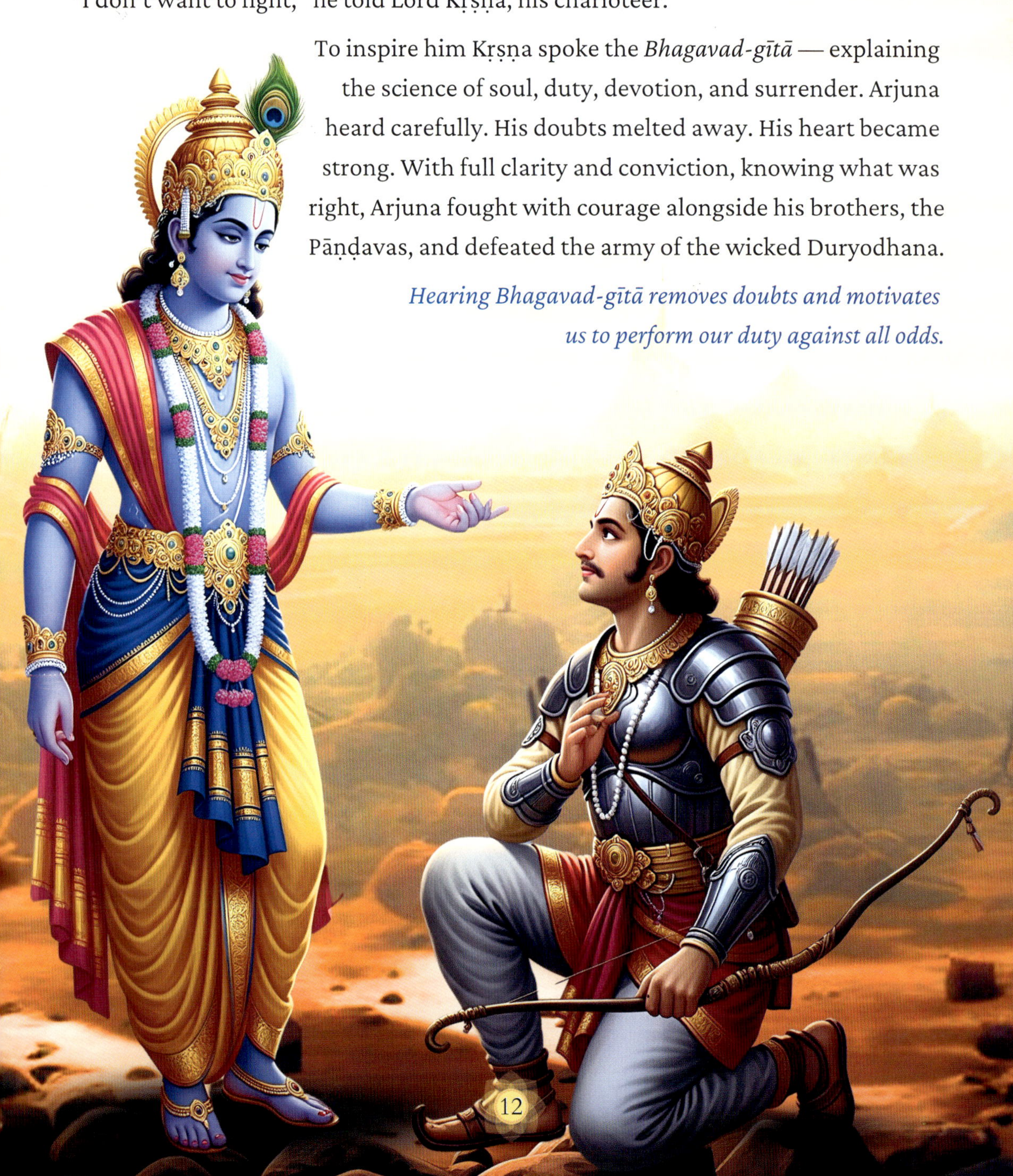

## 3. A Child Becomes Sage Nārada

Long ago, a young boy lived with his mother, a maidservant at a *gurukula*. One year, during the rainy season, saintly devotees known as the *Bhakti-vedāntas* stayed in that area. The boy served them humbly — washing their dishes, bringing them water, and quietly sitting nearby while they spoke about Lord Kṛṣṇa's pastimes and deep spiritual truths.

Their words touched his heart. He felt a kind of happiness he had never known before. When the rainy season ended, the sages initiated the boy and blessed him. Soon after, his mother passed away. The boy then wandered into the forest, meditating on the Lord he had heard about.

At the end of that life, the Lord blessed him with a spiritual body, and he became the great sage Nārada Muni — traveling everywhere, playing his *vīṇā*, and speaking about Kṛṣṇa to all.

*Even a small child who hears sincerely can become a great devotee.*

# 4. Lord Brahmā Creates the Universe

At the dawn of creation, Lord Viṣṇu was resting on the *Garbhodaka* Ocean. From His navel, a gigantic lotus stem grew, and on that lotus appeared Lord Brahmā — the very first created being.

Brahmā looked everywhere. There was only water, stretching endlessly in all directions! Not knowing his identity and duty, Brahmā began to meditate, sincerely praying for guidance.

Pleased with his devotion, the Supreme Lord Kṛṣṇa appeared before him and spoke the essence of the *Śrīmad-Bhāgavatam* in just four special verses, known as the *catuḥ-ślokī.*

Hearing these divine teachings  directly from the Lord, Brahmā became enlightened, joyful, and empowered to conduct his duty of creation. With this wisdom, he was able to create the planets, species, and all living beings in the universe.

*Hearing the Lord's words gives us the clarity and courage to do our duty well.*

## 5. The Wives of the Brāhmaṇas Run to the Forest

Once, Kṛṣṇa and His cowherd friends were playing in the forests of Vṛndāvana when they began to feel hungry. Kṛṣṇa sent some friends to ask nearby brāhmaṇas, who were busy with a sacrifice, for food. But the brāhmaṇas ignored them.

So Kṛṣṇa told His friends to go instead to the brāhmaṇas' wives. As soon as the ladies heard that Kṛṣṇa was nearby and needed food, their hearts leapt with joy. Without a moment's hesitation, they gathered whatever delicious items they had, left their homes, and ran through the forest to meet Him — even though their family members tried to stop them.

How did they develop such eagerness? They had often heard about Kṛṣṇa's beauty, kindness, and pastimes from beetle nut selling girls of Vraja who visited their homes. Just by hearing, they had fallen in love with Him. Now, the chance to serve Him was like a dream come true.

*Hearing about Kṛṣṇa makes us so eager to see and serve Him that nothing can hold us back.*

# 6. King Parīkṣit Goes to the Spiritual World

One day, while hunting, King Parīkṣit felt very thirsty. He came to the *āśrama* of Sage Śamīka and asked for water. The sage was deeply absorbed in meditation and didn't respond. Feeling insulted, the king picked up a dead snake and placed it around the sage's neck as a prank. When the sage's young son Sringi heard about this, he became angry and cursed Parīkṣit to die in seven days, bitten by a snake-bird.

King Parīkṣit accepted the curse calmly. He left his palace, went to the bank of River Ganga. He just desired to hear the topics of Lord Hari in the remaining one week of his life. He expressed his desire to the sages who assembled on the bank of Ganga.

At that time, the great sage Śukadeva Goswami arrived there. Parīkṣit humbly asked him, "What should a person hear, chant and remember throughout one's life and at the time of death?" In response, Śukadeva Goswami narrated *Śrīmad-Bhāgavatam* that elaborately describes the science of Bhakti and the pastimes of Lord Kṛṣṇa and His incarnations. For seven days and nights, the king listened without distraction. On the seventh day, when the snake-bird came, Parīkṣit left his body completely absorbed in thoughts of Kṛṣṇa — and went to the spiritual world.

*Even a short time spent hearing with full*
*attention can lead us to perfection.*

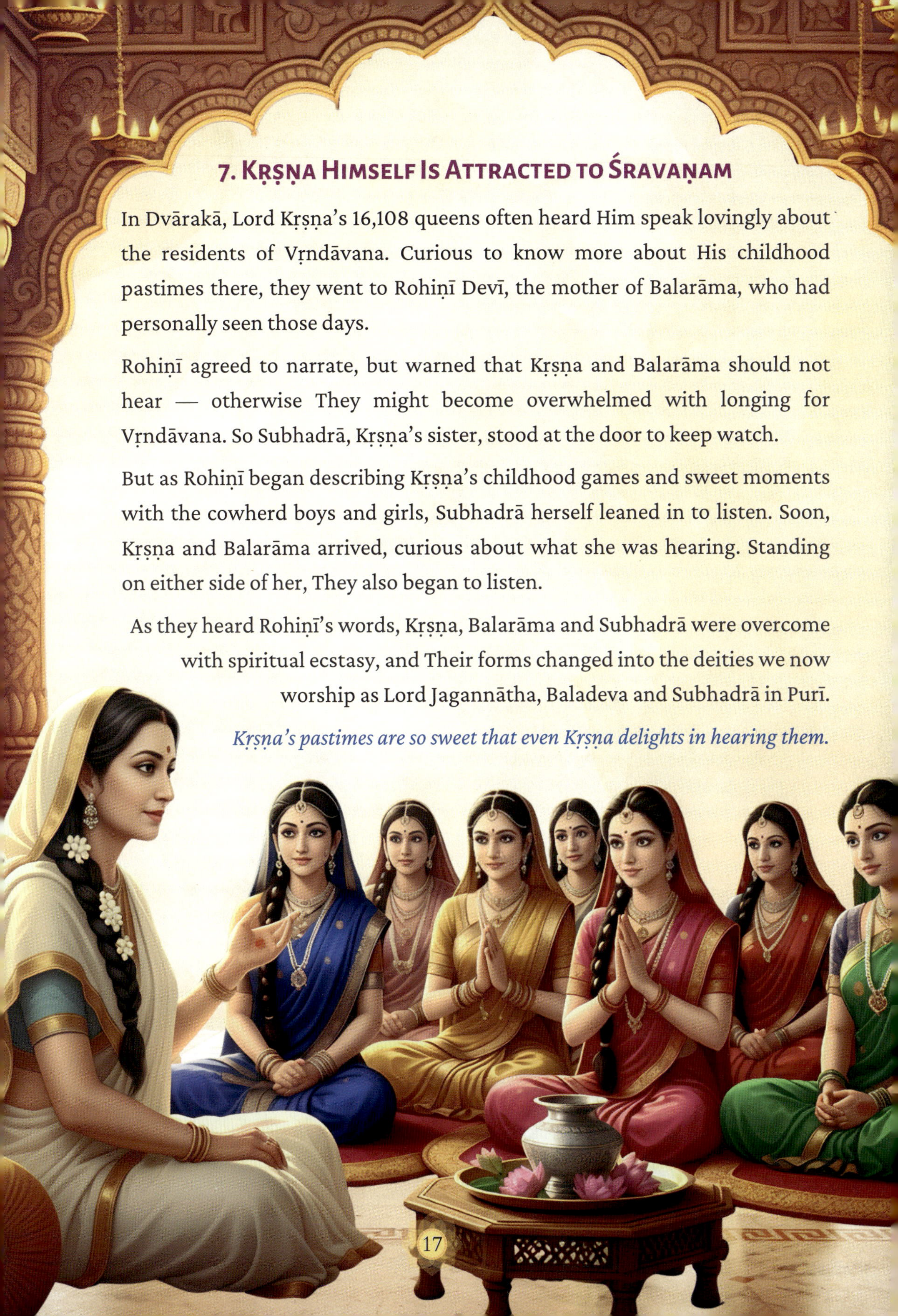

## 7. Kṛṣṇa Himself Is Attracted to Śravaṇam

In Dvārakā, Lord Kṛṣṇa's 16,108 queens often heard Him speak lovingly about the residents of Vṛndāvana. Curious to know more about His childhood pastimes there, they went to Rohiṇī Devī, the mother of Balarāma, who had personally seen those days.

Rohiṇī agreed to narrate, but warned that Kṛṣṇa and Balarāma should not hear — otherwise They might become overwhelmed with longing for Vṛndāvana. So Subhadrā, Kṛṣṇa's sister, stood at the door to keep watch.

But as Rohiṇī began describing Kṛṣṇa's childhood games and sweet moments with the cowherd boys and girls, Subhadrā herself leaned in to listen. Soon, Kṛṣṇa and Balarāma arrived, curious about what she was hearing. Standing on either side of her, They also began to listen.

As they heard Rohiṇī's words, Kṛṣṇa, Balarāma and Subhadrā were overcome with spiritual ecstasy, and Their forms changed into the deities we now worship as Lord Jagannātha, Baladeva and Subhadrā in Purī.

*Kṛṣṇa's pastimes are so sweet that even Kṛṣṇa delights in hearing them.*

# Let's Hear!

*Śravaṇam* can inspire devotion in children, adults, sages, kings, devatas — anyone from any background — and fill the heart with spiritual joy. Whether it is Lord Brahmā at the dawn of creation, Princess Rukmiṇī in her royal palace, Prince Arjuna on the battlefield, the young boy who became Nārada Muni, the sages of Naimiṣāraṇya, or even the Supreme Lord Himself — everyone is attracted and enlivened by *śravaṇam*. That's why we should make a habit of hearing about the Lord every day.

Even Lord Caitanya Mahāprabhu loved to hear the *Śrīmad-Bhāgavatam* from Gadādhara Paṇḍita. If such great personalities relish hearing again and again, we can too.

## Benefits of Hearing about Kṛṣṇa

| 1 | **Illumination** | We gain a clear understanding of spiritual truths. |
|---|---|---|
| 2 | **Purification** | Fear, sorrow, envy, pride, and confusion melt away. |
| 3 | **Emotion** | Our love for Kṛṣṇa increases and becomes steady. |
| 4 | **Action** | We feel inspired to serve the Lord with enthusiasm. |
| 5 | **Reaction** | We face life's challenges with calmness and maturity. |
| 6 | **Relation** | We see others as spiritual beings and respect them. |

1
Listen to a devotional story each day before going to bed and early morning.

2
Ask elders to share their favourite pastimes of Krsna.

3
Attend satsanga or temple lectures regularly.

SIMPLE WAYS TO PRACTICE ŚRAVAṆAM

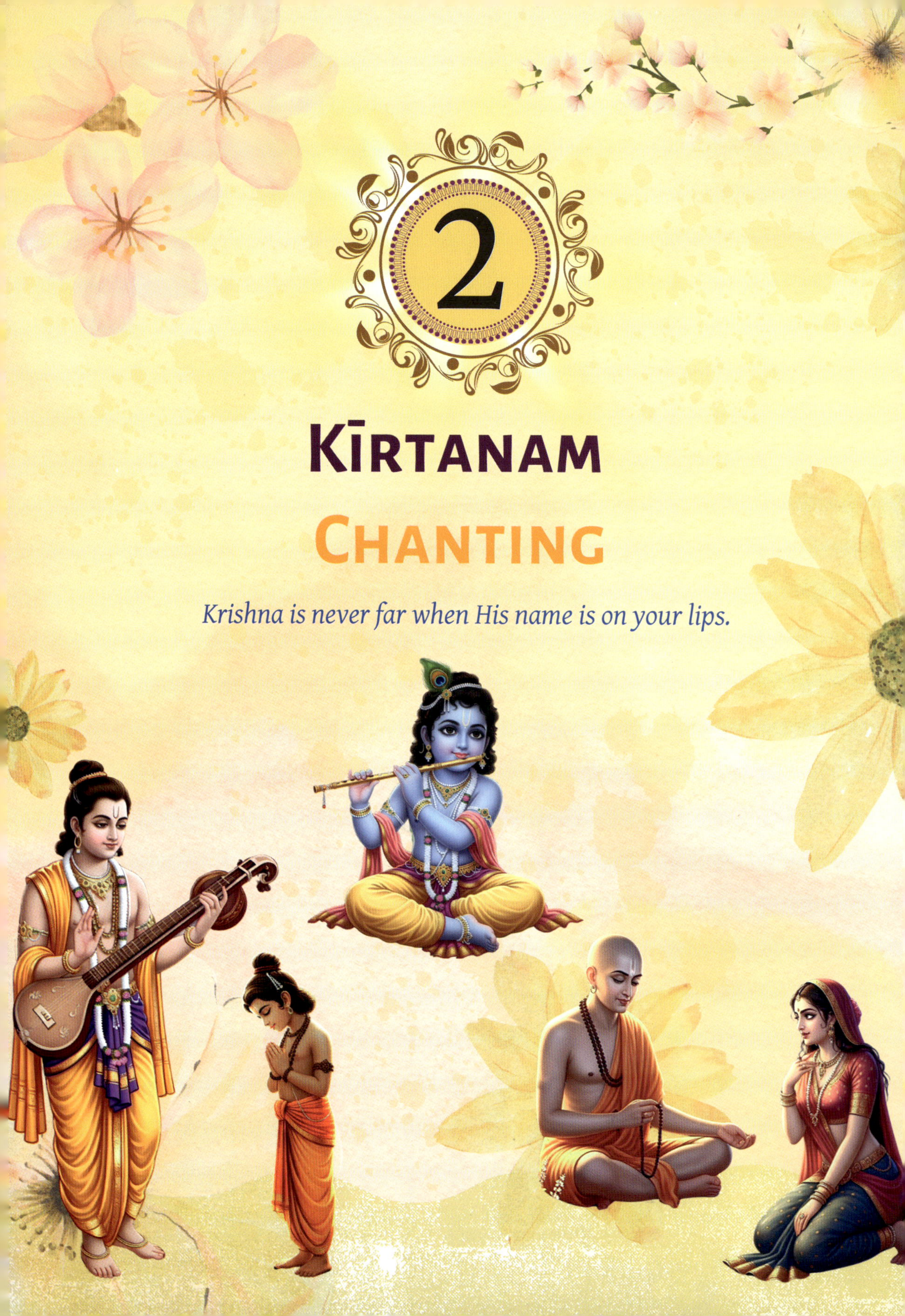


# Kīrtanam

## Chanting

*Krishna is never far when His name is on your lips.*

*Kīrti* means "glory" — the wonderful things that make someone special and praiseworthy.

*Kīrtanam* means "glorifying" — speaking, singing, or chanting those glories so that others can hear and feel inspired.

So, *Kṛṣṇa-kīrtanam* is the joyful process of chanting and glorifying Kṛṣṇa's sweet names, adventurous pastimes, and beautiful qualities — sometimes through singing and sometimes through speaking, but always with love.

*Kīrtanam* is a natural extension of *śravaṇam* (hearing). When we hear about the Lord, our hearts feel happy, and that happiness naturally flows out in the form of *kīrtanam* — by sharing what we heard through singing, chanting, or speaking.

| DIFFERENT KINDS OF KĪRTANAM: | |
| --- | --- |
| 1 NĀMA-KĪRTANAM | Chanting or singing Kṛṣṇa's holy names. |
| 2 RŪPA-KĪRTANAM | Lovingly describing His divine forms. |
| 3 GUṆA-KĪRTANAM | Glorifying His wonderful qualities. |
| 4 LĪLĀ-KĪRTANAM | Praising His enchanting pastimes. |

In this present age of *Kali*, people live short lives, get disturbed easily, and often forget spiritual life. Sacrifices, tough austerities, and long rituals that were practiced in earlier ages are very difficult now. That's why the scriptures again and again recommend *kīrtanam* — glorification of Lord Hari — as the easiest and most powerful method for *Kali-yuga*. *(kalau tad dhari-kīrtanāt).*

The *Śrīmad-Bhāgavatam* (12.3.51) says:

*kaler doṣa-nidhe rājann asti hy eko mahān guṇaḥ*
*kīrtanād eva kṛṣṇasya mukta-saṅgaḥ paraṁ vrajet*

"This age of Kali is an ocean of faults, but it has one great quality. Simply by glorifying Kṛṣṇa, one becomes free from bondage and goes back to the spiritual world."

That is the power of *kīrtanam*! No matter who we are — rich or poor, young or old, strong or weak, educated or uneducated — everyone can take part in this joyful practice. Therefore Lord Kṛṣṇa says: "*satatam kīrtayanto mām* — always glorify Me." (BG 9.14)

And of all types of *kīrtanam, nāma-kīrtanam* (chanting Kṛṣṇa's holy names) is the highest and most powerful, especially in this age.

The *Śrīmad-Bhāgavatam* (2.1.11) confirms:

*etan nirvidyamānānām icchatām akuto-bhayam*
*yogināṁ nṛpa nirṇītaṁ harer nāmānukīrtanam*

"It has been concluded by several great yogis that for one who desires fearlessness in this world — the best path is to chant and glorify the holy name of Lord Hari."

By chanting the Lord's holy names, anyone can become pure at heart, fearless, joyful, and finally return to Kṛṣṇa's eternal home. Here are some shining examples of devotees who perfected their lives through *Kīrtanam*.

**DID YOU KNOW?**

*Kīrtanam* is not about having a good voice or knowing music. It's about singing with enthusiasm and affection. And when we glorify Kṛṣṇa with devotion, the Lord personally listens, smiles, and dances in our hearts.

# 1. Lava and Kuśa Spread the Glories of Rāma

Lord Rāma's twin sons, Lava and Kuśa, grew up in the peaceful hermitage of Sage Vālmīki. From their earliest childhood, they were trained in music, poetry, and devotion. Most importantly, Sage Vālmīki lovingly taught them the *Rāmāyaṇa* — the great story of Lord Rāma.

With their sweet, melodious voices, Lava and Kuśa began singing the *Rāmāyaṇa* in villages, towns, and royal courts. Whoever heard their kīrtana was spellbound. People felt as if they were witnessing Lord Rāma's adventures right before their eyes.

One day, they sang in the royal court of Ayodhyā itself, before King Rāma — not knowing that He was their own father! The entire assembly was enchanted. Even Lord Rāma and His ministers were moved by the depth of devotion shining through the boys' voices.

*Even children can inspire the whole world by glorifying the Lord sincerely.*

## 2. Nārada Muni Sings Across the Worlds

Nārada Muni, the eternal traveling sage, is always seen carrying his vīṇā and singing the Lord's glories. He wanders everywhere — heavenly planets, earthly cities, deep forests, and hermitages. His kīrtanam awakens devotion in the hearts of all who hear him — kings and common people, saints and sinners alike. Even those who are far from spiritual life feel touched and transformed by his *kīrtanam*.

Nārada's *kīrtana* has changed many lives. When he spoke to Kayādhu, the pregnant wife of the demon Hiraṇyakaśipu, the child within her womb absorbed his words of devotion, and became the most celebrated devotee Prahlāda. Nārada Muni also taught the mantra *oṁ namo bhagavate vāsudevāya* to young Dhruva, helping him attain the Lord's darśana at the age of five. He inspired the Pracetas, the sons of King Prācīnabarhi, and also guided the Haryaśvas and Savalāśvas, the sons of Dakṣa, onto the path of devotion. Most importantly, it was Nārada who inspired Vyāsadeva to compose the Śrīmad-Bhāgavatam in its present form.

*Kīrtanam* can be performed anywhere, anytime, and by anyone. You don't need a big stage or a large audience. All you need is a heart full of love for the Lord.

*Kīrtanam is a gift we can share with all*
*living beings, no matter where we are.*

Śukadeva Gosvāmī, the son of Vyāsadeva, was a pure-hearted devotee deeply attracted to the qualities of Lord Hari. From his father, he learned the *Śrīmad-Bhāgavatam*, and with great love, he carried its message in his heart.

Later, when King Parīkṣit was cursed to die within seven days, he left his palace and sat by the River Gaṅgā, desiring only to hear about Lord Hari. Śukadeva Gosvāmī arrived there, and with a prayerful and compassionate heart, he began narrating the Bhāgavatam — the ultimate *kīrtanam*.

For seven days and nights, Śukadeva Gosvāmī described the pastimes of Kṛṣṇa, the glories of His incarnations, the lives of His devotees, and the truths of *bhakti*. Just as the flavor of a ripe fruit becomes even sweeter when touched by a parrot's beak, the pastimes of the Lord became more relishable when narrated by Śukadeva Gosvāmī with deep devotion. The greater the love of the speaker, the greater the love awakened in the hearers.

By listening to this *kīrtanam,* King Parīkṣit became fearless, joyful, and fully absorbed in thoughts of Kṛṣṇa. At the end of the seven days, he left his body completely immersed in devotion and attained liberation.

*When exalted devotees glorify the Lord, their words fill the hearer's heart with pure love for Kṛṣṇa.*

# 4. Vrajavāsīs: The Residents of Vṛndāvana

The *Vrajavāsīs*, are the best examples of those who constantly glorify Kṛṣṇa and sing about His pastimes. For them, every conversation, every activity, and every moment of life is centered on Kṛṣṇa. They have no other topic to discuss or think about!

The cowherd boys begin their day by joyfully singing about Kṛṣṇa's adventures as they take the cows into the forests of Vṛndāvana. In the evening, when they return, they eagerly narrate to Nanda Maharaja and other cowherd men, all of Kṛṣṇa's playful acts and victories — especially how He defeated the demons. Though dangers came almost every day, the cowherd men and the boys never felt disturbed, because their hearts were absorbed in *Kṛṣṇa-kīrtana*.

*When one is absorbed in glorifying Kṛṣṇa, worldly troubles lose their power to disturb.*

Mother Yaśodā, while churning butter for her darling child, sings sweet songs describing His playful childhood pastimes. The motherly *gopīs* also relish Kṛṣṇa's butter-stealing pranks. They prepare fresh butter and milk products hoping Kṛṣṇa would come to 'steal' them, and then gather together to discuss His mischief. Often, they would go to Mother Yaśodā with mock complaints: "Your son has stolen butter from our houses again!" Externally, they seemed to scold Kṛṣṇa, but internally, they overflowed with love. Kṛṣṇa enjoyed this special form of kīrtana even more than the chanting of Vedic mantras!

The gopīs had another sweet intention behind their complaints. They wanted Mother Yaśodā, who might miss these secret butter-stealing adventures, to hear about them and share in their joy. Hearing their words, Yaśodā experienced a happiness even greater than the gopīs who directly saw those acts.

This is the unique nature of Kṛṣṇa's enchanting līlās: *When narrated by pure devotees like the gopīs or Śukadeva Gosvāmī, they become even more nectarean, because they are mixed with the love of the speaker.*

The younger *gopīs* also sang constantly of Kṛṣṇa. Together they composed songs like the *Veṇu-gīta* (describing the beauty of His flute-playing), the *Yugala-gīta* (about His wanderings in the forest and how even the animals became enchanted), and the *Gopī-gīta* (songs of deep longing in separation from Him).

The women of *Vraja* are described as the most fortunate, because with hearts fully absorbed in Kṛṣṇa and voices often choked with tears, they sang about Him in all their daily chores — milking cows, winnowing grain, churning butter, gathering cow dung, swinging on swings, sprinkling water, or cleaning their homes. Every activity of life was filled with *Kṛṣṇa-kīrtanam*.

*We don't need a special place or time for kīrtanam.*
*Whether working, playing, or resting, we can keep chanting in the background.*

# 5. Lord Caitanya Inspires Animals and Birds to Chant!

Hearing the holy name is already powerful, but chanting it aloud makes its effect even stronger. When we chant softly, it purifies our own heart, but when we chant loudly, it blesses everyone around us — even trees, birds, animals, and insects! Lord Caitanya Mahāprabhu showed the same miracle. While traveling through the dense forest of Jhārikhaṇḍa, He chanted "Kṛṣṇa! Kṛṣṇa!" so loudly and sweetly that even tigers, elephants, deer, monkeys, and birds began to chant along with Him! The trees too seemed to echo the holy name.

*Loud kīrtanam can benefit even animals, birds, and trees!*

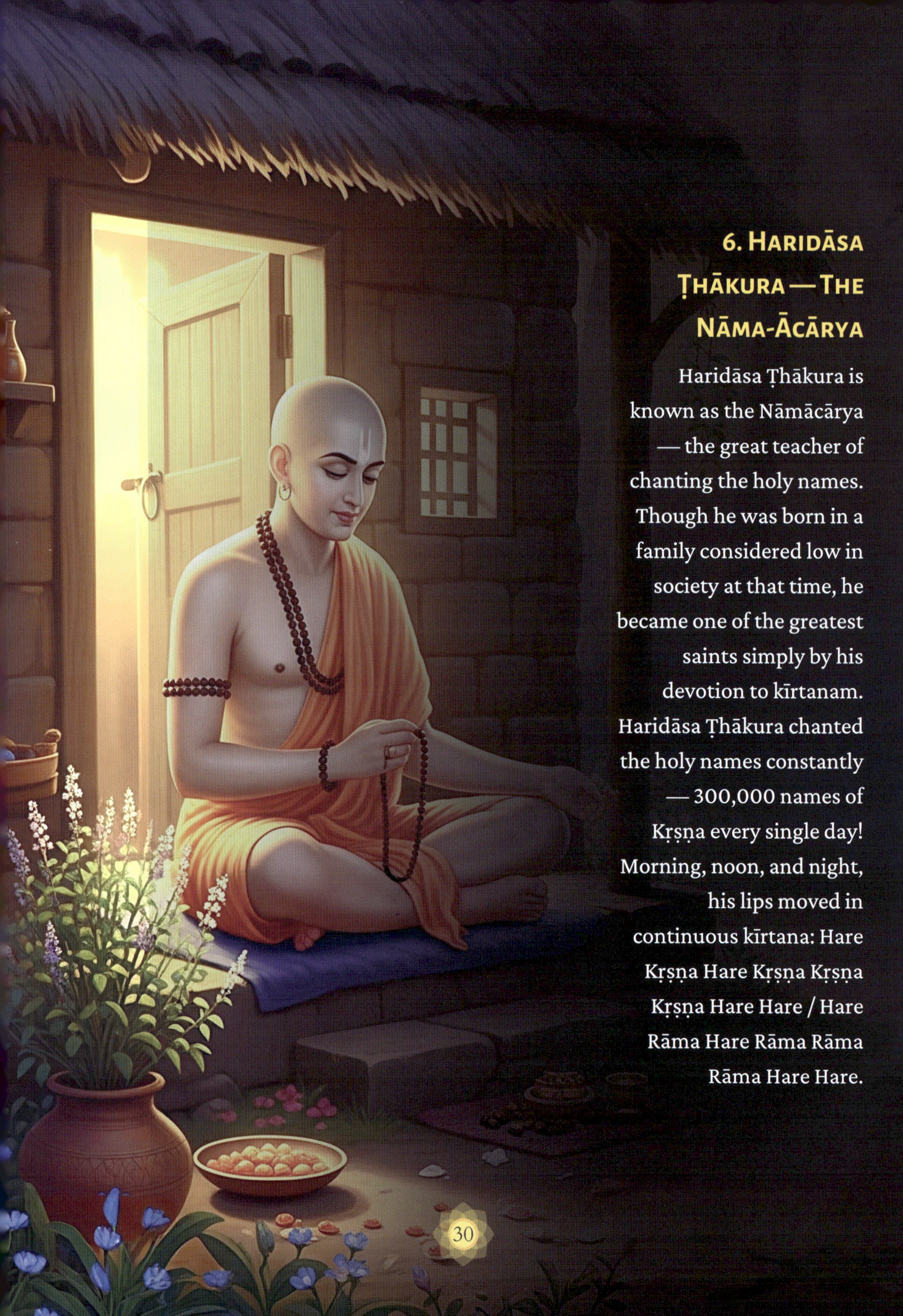

## 6. Haridāsa Ṭhākura — The Nāma-Ācārya

Haridāsa Ṭhākura is known as the Nāmācārya — the great teacher of chanting the holy names. Though he was born in a family considered low in society at that time, he became one of the greatest saints simply by his devotion to kīrtanam. Haridāsa Ṭhākura chanted the holy names constantly — 300,000 names of Kṛṣṇa every single day! Morning, noon, and night, his lips moved in continuous kīrtana: Hare Kṛṣṇa Hare Kṛṣṇa Kṛṣṇa Kṛṣṇa Hare Hare / Hare Rāma Hare Rāma Rāma Rāma Hare Hare.

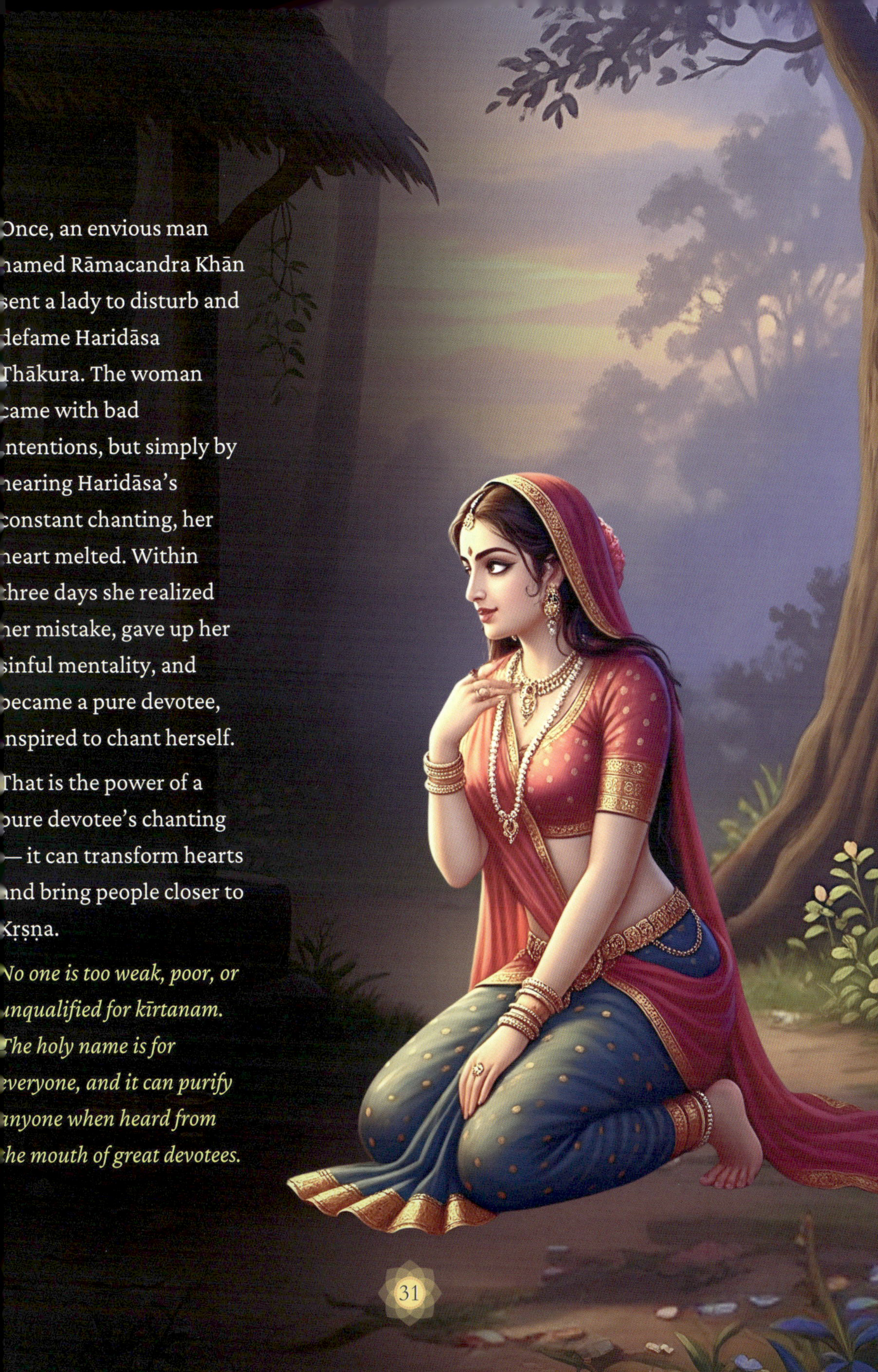

Once, an envious man named Rāmacandra Khān sent a lady to disturb and defame Haridāsa Thākura. The woman came with bad intentions, but simply by hearing Haridāsa's constant chanting, her heart melted. Within three days she realized her mistake, gave up her sinful mentality, and became a pure devotee, inspired to chant herself.

That is the power of a pure devotee's chanting — it can transform hearts and bring people closer to Kṛṣṇa.

No one is too weak, poor, or unqualified for kīrtanam. The holy name is for everyone, and it can purify anyone when heard from the mouth of great devotees.

# 7. Śrīla Prabhupāda Starts a Worldwide Sankīrtana Movement

At the age of 69, when most people think of retiring, Śrīla A.C. Bhaktivedanta Swami Prabhupāda left the sacred land of Vṛndāvana and traveled alone to America — a faraway country with a very different culture. He carried just a small suitcase, a few books, and a pair of *kartālas* (hand cymbals) and an unshakable faith in the holy name of Kṛṣṇa.

After weeks on a rough sea voyage, he arrived in New York City. He had no money, no friends, and no followers. But he had the greatest treasures: *Śrīmad-Bhāgavatam* and Kṛṣṇa's holy name.

Śrīla Prabhupāda began lecturing to whoever came to hear about Kṛṣṇa from him. He started chanting Hare Kṛṣṇa in Tompkins Square Park. At first, only a few curious young people stopped to watch the elderly saint singing with closed eyes, playing his *kartālas*, and dancing softly. But the sound of the *mahā-mantra* was so pure, so filled with spiritual power, that soon more people joined in. They clapped, sang, and danced with him. The crowd grew bigger and bigger.

Day after day, the chanting spread. Young seekers, musicians, students, and even ordinary passers-by felt touched in their hearts. They had never heard anything like it. Some said they felt real peace for the first time in their lives.

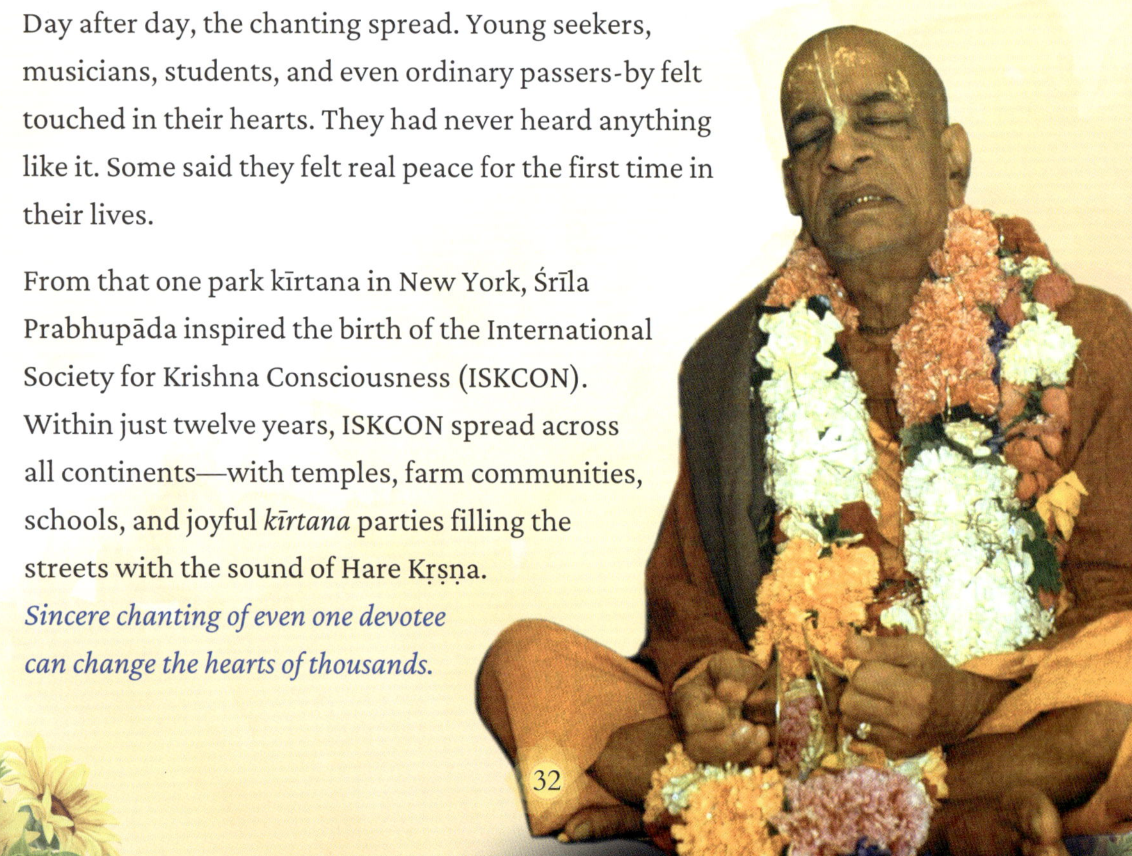

From that one park kīrtana in New York, Śrīla Prabhupāda inspired the birth of the International Society for Krishna Consciousness (ISKCON). Within just twelve years, ISKCON spread across all continents—with temples, farm communities, schools, and joyful *kīrtana* parties filling the streets with the sound of Hare Kṛṣṇa.

*Sincere chanting of even one devotee can change the hearts of thousands.*

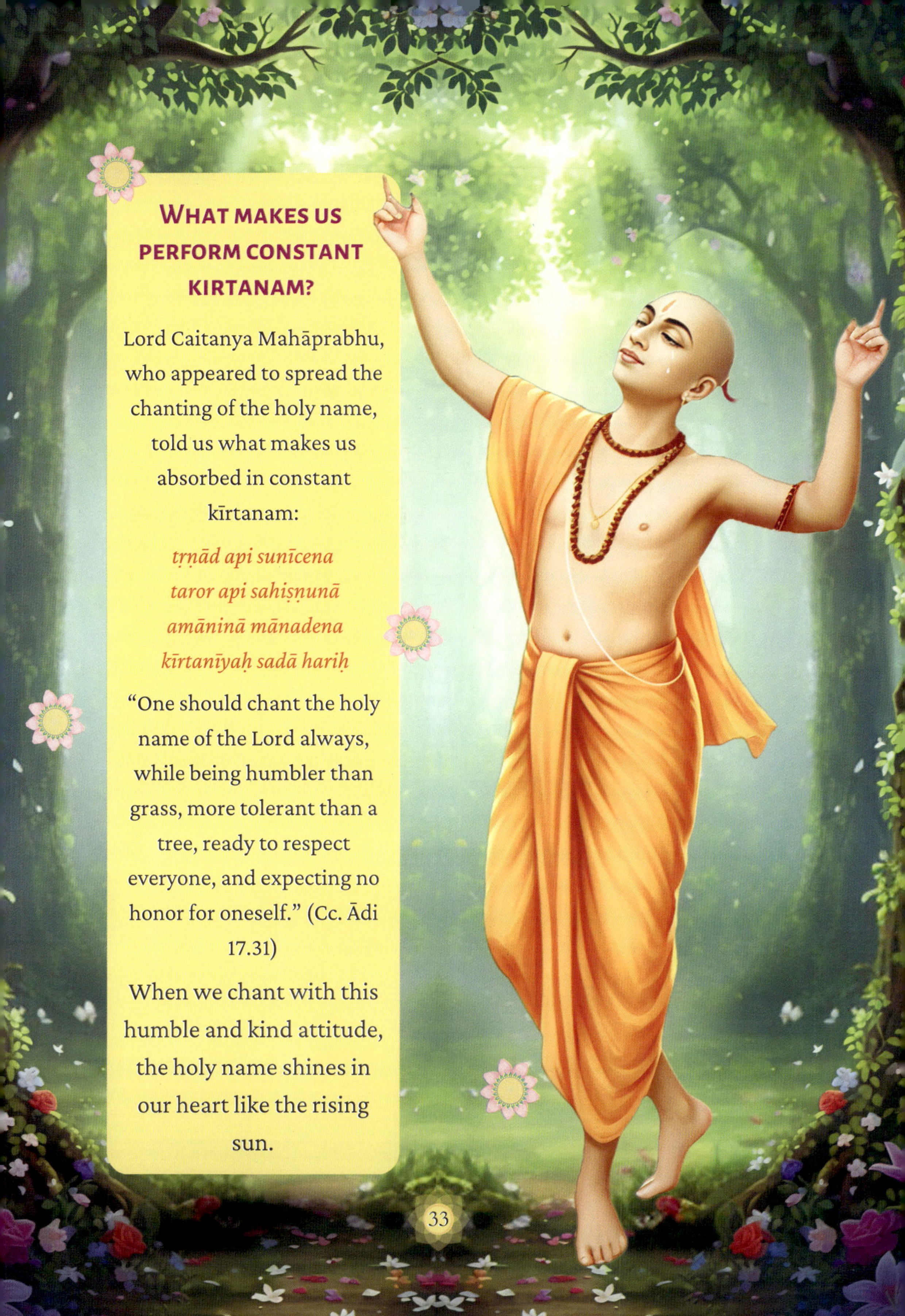

## What makes us perform constant kirtanam?

Lord Caitanya Mahāprabhu, who appeared to spread the chanting of the holy name, told us what makes us absorbed in constant kīrtanam:

*tṛṇād api sunīcena*
*taror api sahiṣṇunā*
*amāninā mānadena*
*kīrtanīyaḥ sadā hariḥ*

"One should chant the holy name of the Lord always, while being humbler than grass, more tolerant than a tree, ready to respect everyone, and expecting no honor for oneself." (Cc. Ādi 17.31)

When we chant with this humble and kind attitude, the holy name shines in our heart like the rising sun.

# Let's Sing!

*Kīrtanam* is a treasure that anyone can practice — children or elders, kings or sages, saints or ordinary people, even animals and birds! From Nārada Muni who sang across the worlds, to Śukadeva and Sūta Gosvāmī who inspired thousands through the *Bhāgavatam*, from the *Vrajavāsīs* of Vṛndāvana to Haridāsa Ṭhākura's fearless chanting, from Lava and Kuśa's sweet *Rāmāyaṇa* songs to Lord Caitanya's miracle of making animals chant, and finally Śrīla Prabhupāda spreading *kīrtana* worldwide — the message is clear: *kīrtanam* transforms hearts and fills the world with spiritual bliss.

That's why we should make *kīrtanam* part of our daily life. Even if we sing softly, loudly, alone, or in a group — the holy names and glories of Kṛṣṇa awaken devotion in our hearts. And by sharing it, we spread that devotion everywhere.

## Benefits of Kīrtanam

| | | |
|---|---|---|
| 1 | **Purification** | Cleanses the heart of fear, anger, envy, and pride. |
| 2 | **Illumination** | Awakens remembrance of Kṛṣṇa and His pastimes. |
| 3 | **Inspiration** | Fills us with enthusiasm to serve the Lord joyfully. |
| 4 | **Connection** | Brings unity and love when sung together with others. |
| 5 | **Liberation** | Frees us from material bondage and leads us back to Kṛṣṇa. |
| 6 | **Transformation** | Even the hardest hearts can be softened by hearing the holy names and pastimes of the Lord. |

SIMPLE WAYS TO PRACTICE KĪRTANAM

1
Chant or sing the *Hare Kṛṣṇa mahā-mantra* daily, even for a few minutes.

2
Sing *kīrtana* with family or friends — clap, play instruments, and dance together.

3
Narrate your favorite stories of Kṛṣṇa to your friends.

4
Join *kīrtanas* in temples or satsang sessions to experience the joy of group chanting.

5
Make chores joyful! Sing or hum Kṛṣṇa's names, songs or verses while walking, bathing, or doing household work.

6
Write and share your own little songs glorifying Kṛṣṇa, just like the *Vrajavāsīs* and Lava–Kuśa.

# Smaraṇam

## Remembering

*What we keep in our mind, shapes what we become. So let's keep Kṛṣṇa there!*

*Smaraṇam* means remembering the Supreme Lord in our heart. It is like keeping Kṛṣṇa always by our side, even when we cannot see Him.

Hearing about the Lord (*śravaṇam*) and chanting His glories (*kīrtanam*) naturally lead us to remembrance (*smaraṇam*). Think about when you hear or sing your favorite song at an event — even after the event ends, the tune keeps playing in your mind, right? That's exactly what smaraṇam means: constant remembrance. It's letting Kṛṣṇa's names, forms, and pastimes keep "playing in your heart" all the time. This is the essence of spiritual life.

The *Padma Purāṇa* says:

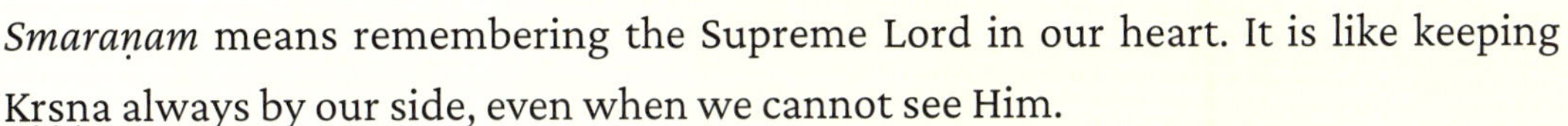

*smartavyaḥ satataṁ viṣṇuḥ vismartavyo na jātucit*
*sarve vidhi-niṣedhāḥ syur etayor eva kiṅkarāḥ*

"Always remember Viṣṇu, and never forget Him. All other rules of the scriptures are servants of these two instructions."

This shows that remembering the Lord is not just one practice of devotion — it is actually the heart of *bhakti*.

In the *Bhagavad-gītā*, Kṛṣṇa again and again tells us to remember Him:

- 9.34: *man-manā bhava mad-bhakto* — "Always think of Me."
- 12.8: *mayy eva mana ādhatsva* — "Fix your mind upon Me."
- 8.7: *tasmāt sarveṣu kāleṣu mām anusmara* — "Therefore, Arjuna, always remember Me while doing your duty."

Here we see two special promises of Kṛṣṇa in the *Bhagavad-gītā* about remembrance:

## TWO SPECIAL PROMISES OF KRṢṆA

**1** If we remember Him **throughout our life,** He will protect us & take care of everything we need (9.22).

**2** If we remember Him **at the end of life,** He will take us back to His eternal abode (8.5).

This shows how powerful remembrance is! If we practice remembering Kṛṣṇa throughout our life, then at the final moment too, our mind will naturally run towards Him — and He will take us back to His eternal home. But if we remember something else at that time, that is what we will attain. For example:

- The demon Vṛtrāsura, though born in a demonic family, remembered the Lord at death and attained Vaikuṇṭha.
- But Bharata Mahārāja, remembered a deer at the time of death, and in his next life, he became a deer!

Just as we always remember those we love — like our parents, best friends, or a favorite hero — a devotee naturally remembers Kṛṣṇa, the greatest well-wisher and best friend of all living beings.

In this chapter, we will see inspiring examples of devotees — young and old, kings and queens, sages and saints — who perfected their lives through the simple but powerful practice of smaraṇam.

### DID YOU KNOW?

*Smaraṇam* makes every moment of life sacred. If we practice remembering the Lord throughout the day, then at the final moment of our lives we will naturally remember Him — and that remembrance will carry us back to Him forever.

38

# 1. Sītādevī Remembers Rāma in Laṅkā

Sītā-devī, the eternal consort of Lord Rāma, showed the world the power of remembrance. While she and Rāma were living in the forest, the demon king Rāvaṇa disguised himself as a saintly *brāhmaṇa* and kidnapped her. He took her to Laṅkā and arrested her in the Aśoka-vana, guarded by fierce demonesses.

Sītā was far away from her beloved Lord Rāma, but day and night, she remembered Him. She thought of His bow and arrows, His gentle smile, and His loving words. Though she sat on the bare ground, thin and weak, her heart glowed with the light of Rāma's remembrance.

Rāvaṇa tried to tempt her: "Become my queen and you will have the greatest palace, riches, and honor." His guards threatened her with cruel words. But none of this shook her mind. She never forgot Rāma, even for a single moment. Her unbroken remembrance gave her courage until Hanumān leapt into Laṅkā and brought her Rāma's ring — a sign that her Lord was coming. Soon after, Rāma killed Rāvaṇa, and Sītā was joyfully reunited with Him.

*In times of sorrow or loneliness, remembering the Lord gives us courage and hope.*

## 2. Prahlāda Never Forgets the Lord

Prahlāda was just a little boy, but his love for Lord Hari was unshakable. Even before he was born, while still in his mother's womb, he had heard about devotion from Nārada Muni. That is why he came into the world already filled with bhakti!

Prahlāda's mind was always absorbed in remembering Kṛṣṇa. It was as if he was captured by the "Kṛṣṇa-planet" (*kṛṣṇa-graha gṛhītātmā*) and constantly felt embraced by Lord Govinda (*govinda-parirambhita*). Sometimes he laughed with joy when he felt the Lord's presence. Sometimes he sang loudly in happiness. At other times he cried in separation, or stood still, his eyes brimming with tears and his hair standing on end. His remembrance of Kṛṣṇa was so deep that he hardly noticed whether he was sitting, walking, eating, or talking.

But Prahlāda's father, the demon king Hiraṇyakaśipu, hated Lord Hari. He tried everything to stop his son from remembering the Lord. He threw Prahlāda into fire, had elephants trample him, pushed him off a cliff, and even gave him poison. Yet Prahlāda remained calm, always smiling and remembering his Lord in every danger. His heart never left Kṛṣṇa, not even for a single moment.

Finally, when Hiraṇyakaśipu roared in anger and threatened Prahlāda again, Lord Nṛsiṁhadeva burst out from a pillar — half man and half lion — and destroyed the demon king, protecting His beloved devotee.

*If we remember Kṛṣṇa like Prahlāda, He will always stay by our side and protect us.*

## 3. Vidura and Uddhava Remember Kṛṣṇa

Just before Lord Kṛṣṇa concluded His pastimes and departed from this world, He gave His dear devotee and friend Uddhava many deep and precious teachings. These instructions, known as the Uddhava-gītā, were like a jewel — Kṛṣṇa's final gift of wisdom. After speaking them, Kṛṣṇa told Uddhava to go to Badarikāśrama and share these teachings with the sages there.

On his journey to Badarikāśrama, Uddhava met Vidura, the noble minister of Hastināpura. Vidura had earlier been insulted and banished by the cruel Duryodhana just before the Kurukṣetra war. Since then, Vidura had been traveling through forests and holy places, spending his days remembering Kṛṣṇa.

When Vidura saw Uddhava, his heart leapt in joy. Immediately, he remembered Kṛṣṇa and eagerly asked, "How are the Yadus? Please share the news of my beloved Lord Kṛṣṇa?"

By this time, however, Kṛṣṇa had already departed from this world. Uddhava's heart was overwhelmed. He could not bring himself to answer. Instead, he closed his eyes and for one full muhūrta (48 minutes), he went into deep trance, remembering Kṛṣṇa.

When Uddhava returned to external consciousness, he spoke with tears: "Dear Vidura, what welfare are you asking about? The sun of Kṛṣṇa has already set. The entire Yadu dynasty has left this world. Without my beloved Lord, my heart is torn in separation."

Uddhava then began recalling Kṛṣṇa's countless qualities and pastimes: His compassion for even demons like Pūtanā, His love and obedience to His parents Vasudeva and Devakī, His cleverness in battle — sometimes even playfully running away to protect His devotees.  He remembered His enchanting childhood in Vṛndāvana, His heroic deeds in Mathurā, His victory over Kaṁsa and other demons, His building of the splendid city of Dvārakā, His marriages to 16,108 queens, His guidance to the Pāṇḍavas in the Kurukṣetra war, and finally, His return to His eternal abode.

Listening to Uddhava's remembrance, Vidura felt his heart melt with devotion. Inspired, he requested Uddhava to become his guru. But Uddhava, respecting Vidura as an elder — almost like a father — directed him instead to seek guidance from Maitreya Muni, another great devotee, while he himself continued to Badarikāśrama to carry out Kṛṣṇa's instruction.

*Remembering Kṛṣṇa's pastimes, qualities, teachings, and instructions gives us strength and direction.*

# 4. Arjuna's Ecstatic Smaranam

Mother Kuntī and her five sons — Yudhiṣṭhira, Bhīma, Arjuna, Nakula, and Sahadeva — faced many ups and downs in life. Sometimes they lived in a grand palace surrounded by luxury, and sometimes they wandered in the forest. They fought fierce battles, lost loved ones, and endured long years of exile. But through joy and sorrow, one thing never changed: they always remembered Kṛṣṇa.

When Lord Kṛṣṇa finally concluded His earthly pastimes and returned to His eternal abode, Arjuna's heart was overwhelmed with grief. He sat down and began to remember all the ways Kṛṣṇa had helped them:

"By Kṛṣṇa's mercy, I won Draupadī's hand by piercing the fish target, while hundreds of proud princes failed."

"It was He who gave us victory against mighty kings, and it was His strength that allowed Bhīma to defeat Jarāsandha and rescue the imprisoned kings."

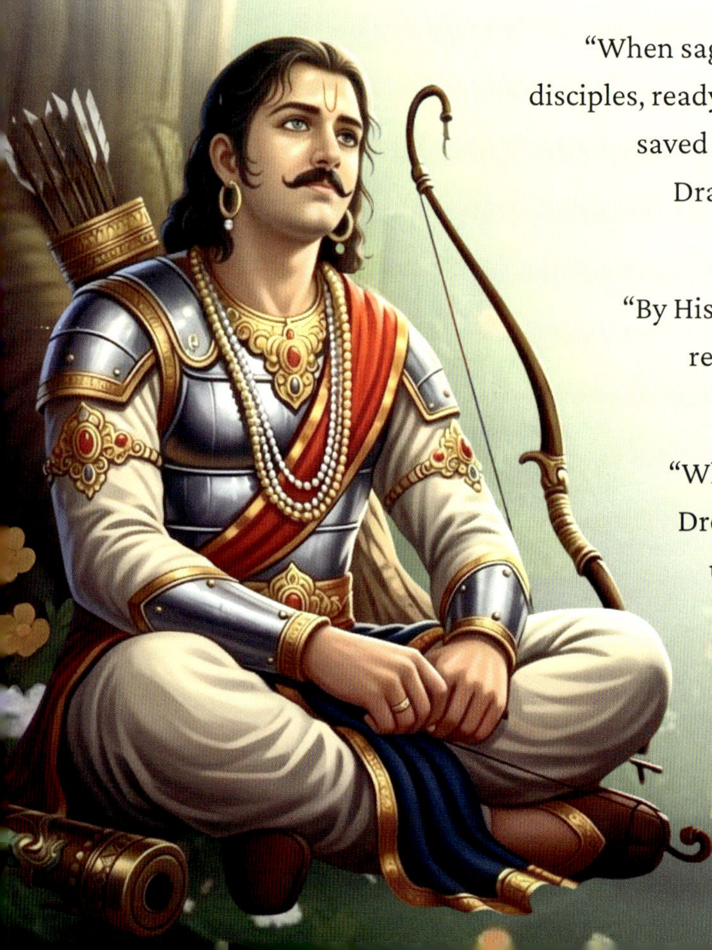

"When sage Durvāsā came with thousands of disciples, ready to curse us during our exile, Kṛṣṇa saved us simply by eating one grain from Draupadī's pot. Everyone felt fully fed and we were saved from danger."

"By His power, I fought Lord Śiva Himself, received celestial weapons, and even sat on Indra's throne."

"When the great generals like Bhīṣma, Droṇa, and Karṇa showered weapons upon me in the Kurukshetra battle, none could touch even by hair, because Kṛṣṇa was with me."

"Even when I foolishly engaged the Supreme Lord as my charioteer, He accepted it with a smile, as if He were my servant."

As Arjuna remembered all these favors, his heart ached in separation. He thought: "I remember His frank talks, His laughter and His loving words. He tolerated all my faults, like a patient father or a kind friend. Now, without Him, my heart feels empty."

Then Arjuna remembered how Krishna motivated him to fight in the Kurukshetra battle by speaking the *Bhagavad Gita.* By remembering those same instructions of the Gita, Arjuna gained composure and focused on his duty after Krishna's departure.

*A devotee always remembers the Lord's favors with gratitude, and remembers His instructions to focus on His service.*

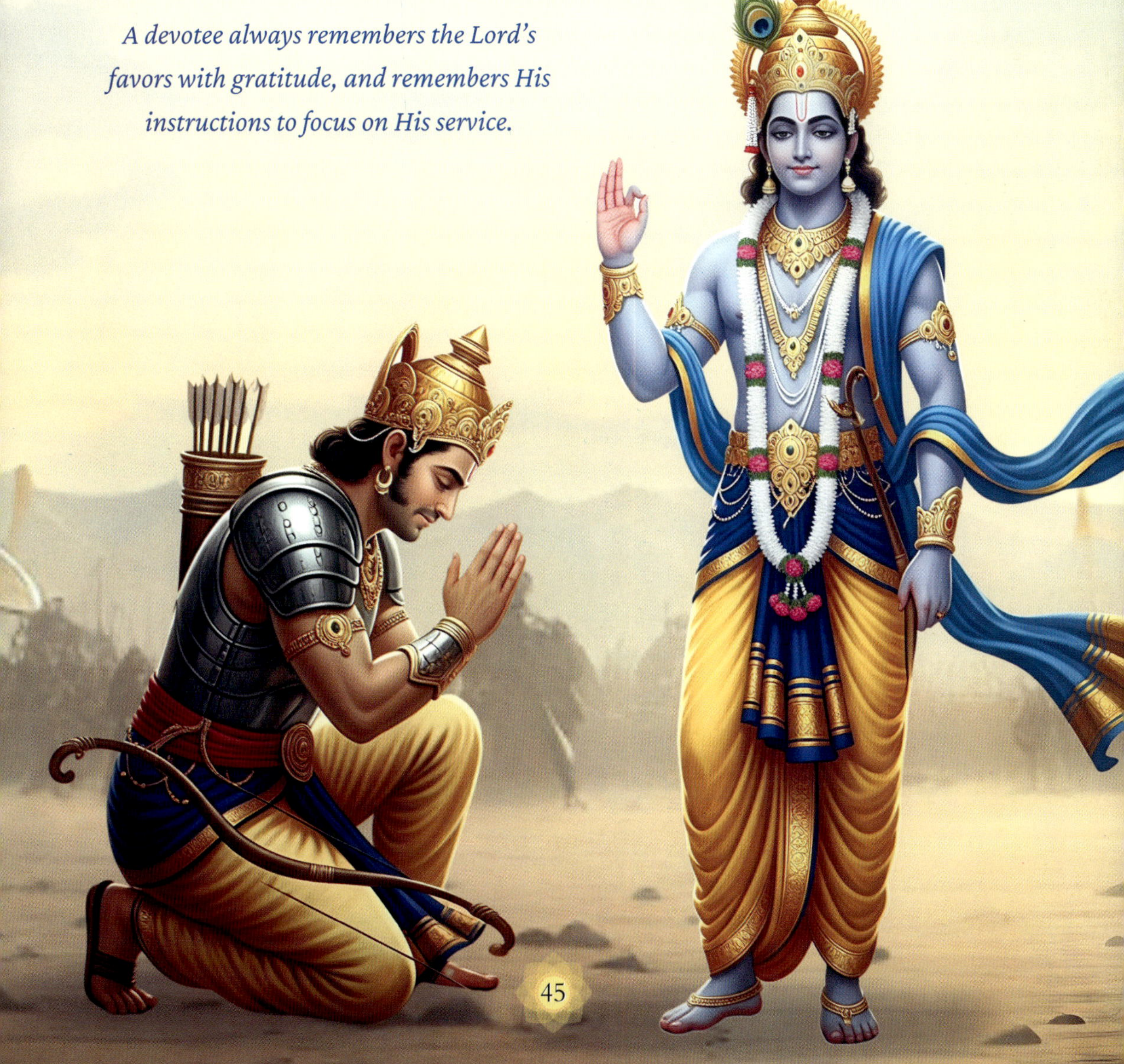

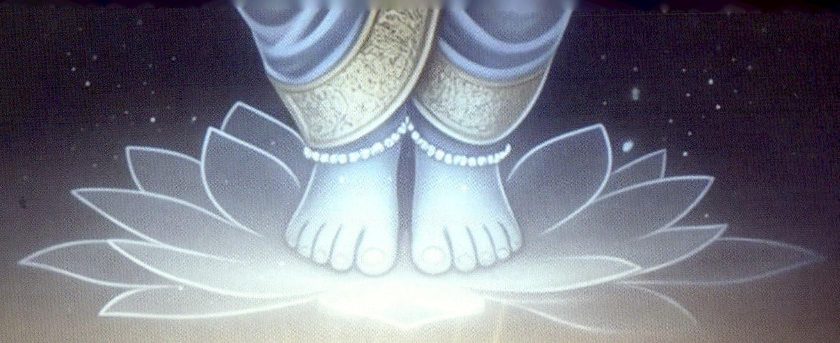

## 5. King Khaṭvāṅga Chooses Remembrance in His Last Minute

Mahārāja Khaṭvāṅga was a powerful and noble king. Once, the devatas invited him to help them in their battle against fierce demons. The king fought bravely and pleased the devatas with his service. Grateful, they offered him a boon of his choice. But instead of asking for riches or pleasures, the king asked a simple question: "How much longer will I live?"

The devatas replied, "Only one muhūrta — forty-eight minutes."

At once, the wise king, without wasting a single moment, fixed his heart completely on the Supreme Lord. With deep love, he remembered Viṣṇu until his final breath. By this remembrance, he attained the spiritual world.

*Even a single moment of sincere remembrance of the Lord can take us back to Him.*

# 6. MOTHER EARTH REMEMBERS KṚṢṆA

After Lord Kṛṣṇa completed His pastimes and left this world, the dark Age of Kali began. At that time, *Dharma* took the form of a bull, and Mother Earth took the form of a cow and met at a place. Both looked very sad. Seeing her grief, *Dharma* asked gently, "Dear Mother, why do you look so unhappy? Is your heart pained because you miss Lord Kṛṣṇa? Are you remembering His pastimes and feeling separation from Him?"

Mother Earth sighed and said, "Yes, I am remembering Him... and that is why I look so sad. Kṛṣṇa is an ocean of wonderful qualities, and my heart aches when I think of them. When He was on earth, He was always truthful, pure, and compassionate. He could not bear to see others suffer. He was steady in mind, equal to all, humble, and filled with wisdom. He was a perfect leader—gracious, efficient, and noble. At the same time, He was joyful, gentle, and very kind.

I was most fortunate when the signs of His lotus feet decorated me with marks of the flag, lotus, thunderbolt, and goad. When He walked upon me, the dust of His feet made me tremble in happiness, just like a person's hairs stand on end when they feel great joy.

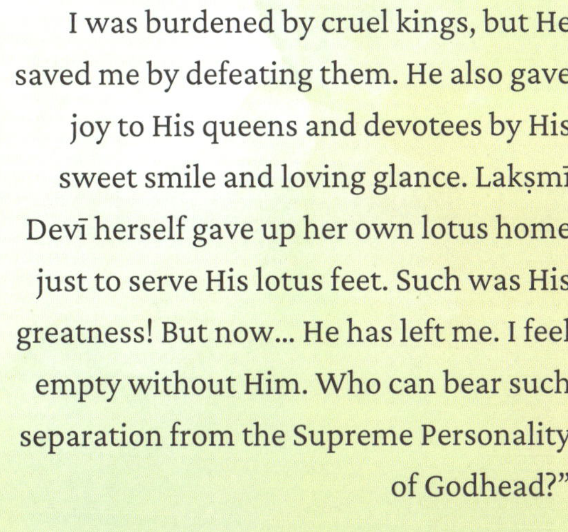

I was burdened by cruel kings, but He saved me by defeating them. He also gave joy to His queens and devotees by His sweet smile and loving glance. Lakṣmī Devī herself gave up her own lotus home just to serve His lotus feet. Such was His greatness! But now... He has left me. I feel empty without Him. Who can bear such separation from the Supreme Personality of Godhead?"

*Smaraṇam is the only solace for a devotee who is feeling separation from Kṛṣṇa.*

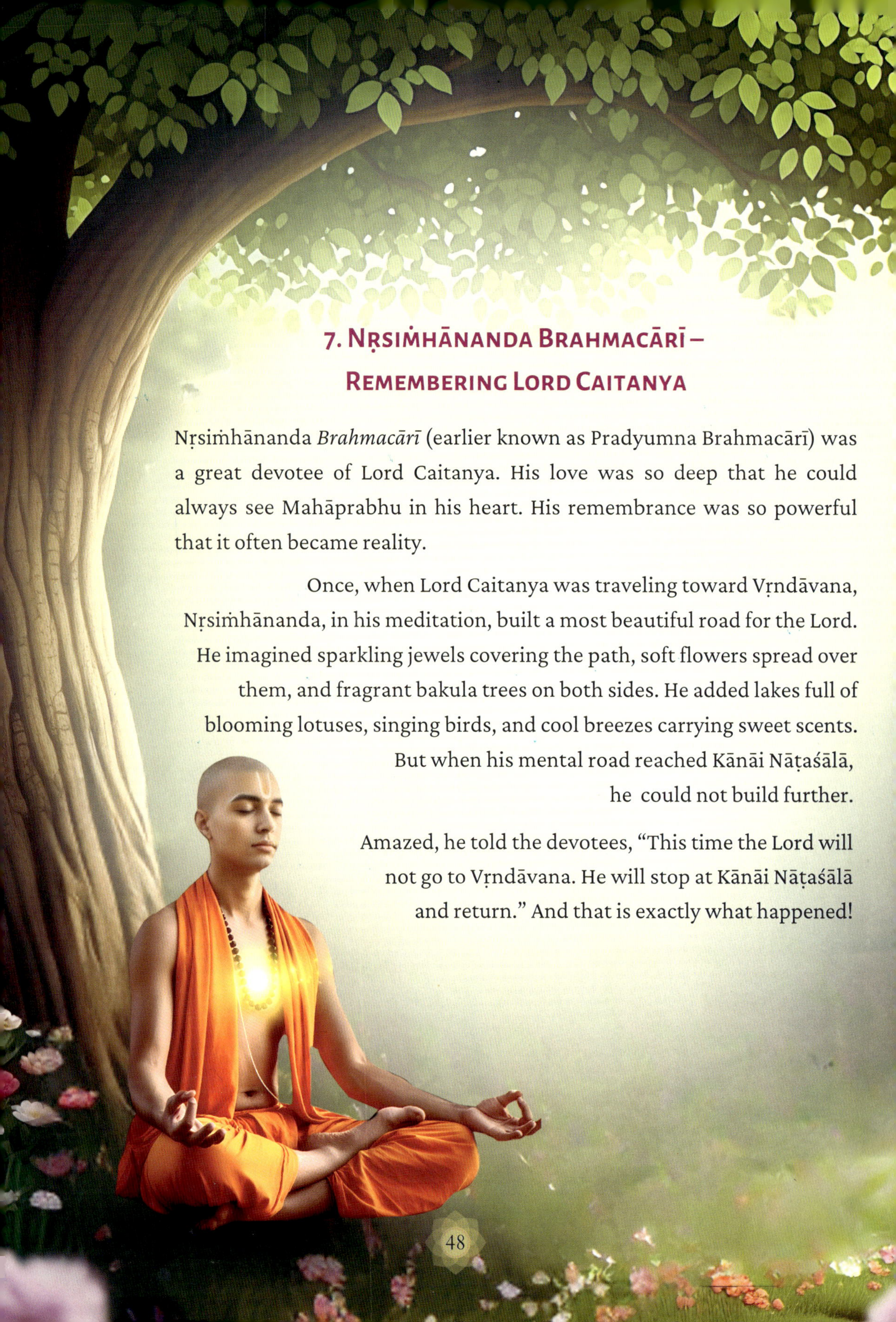

# 7. Nṛsiṁhānanda Brahmacārī –
# Remembering Lord Caitanya

Nṛsiṁhānanda *Brahmacārī* (earlier known as Pradyumna Brahmacārī) was a great devotee of Lord Caitanya. His love was so deep that he could always see Mahāprabhu in his heart. His remembrance was so powerful that it often became reality.

Once, when Lord Caitanya was traveling toward Vṛndāvana, Nṛsiṁhānanda, in his meditation, built a most beautiful road for the Lord. He imagined sparkling jewels covering the path, soft flowers spread over them, and fragrant bakula trees on both sides. He added lakes full of blooming lotuses, singing birds, and cool breezes carrying sweet scents. But when his mental road reached Kānāi Nāṭaśālā, he could not build further.

Amazed, he told the devotees, "This time the Lord will not go to Vṛndāvana. He will stop at Kānāi Nāṭaśālā and return." And that is exactly what happened!

On another occasion, Nṛsiṁhānanda assured the devotees, "Don't worry — Lord Caitanya will come here tomorrow and eat at Śivānanda Sena's house." Though Mahāprabhu was far away, Nṛsiṁhānanda cooked many delicious dishes — rice, vegetables, cakes, and sweets — and offered them in his meditation to Lord Jagannātha, Lord Nṛsiṁhadeva, and Lord Caitanya.

In his heart, he saw Mahāprabhu personally eating all three offerings! Later, in Jagannātha Purī, Lord Caitanya Himself confirmed it, saying, "Last year, Nṛsiṁhānanda cooked for Me such wonderful food that I had never tasted before!"

*A devotee who remembers the Lord deeply can truly feel His presence; and his mental service is accepted as real by the Lord.*

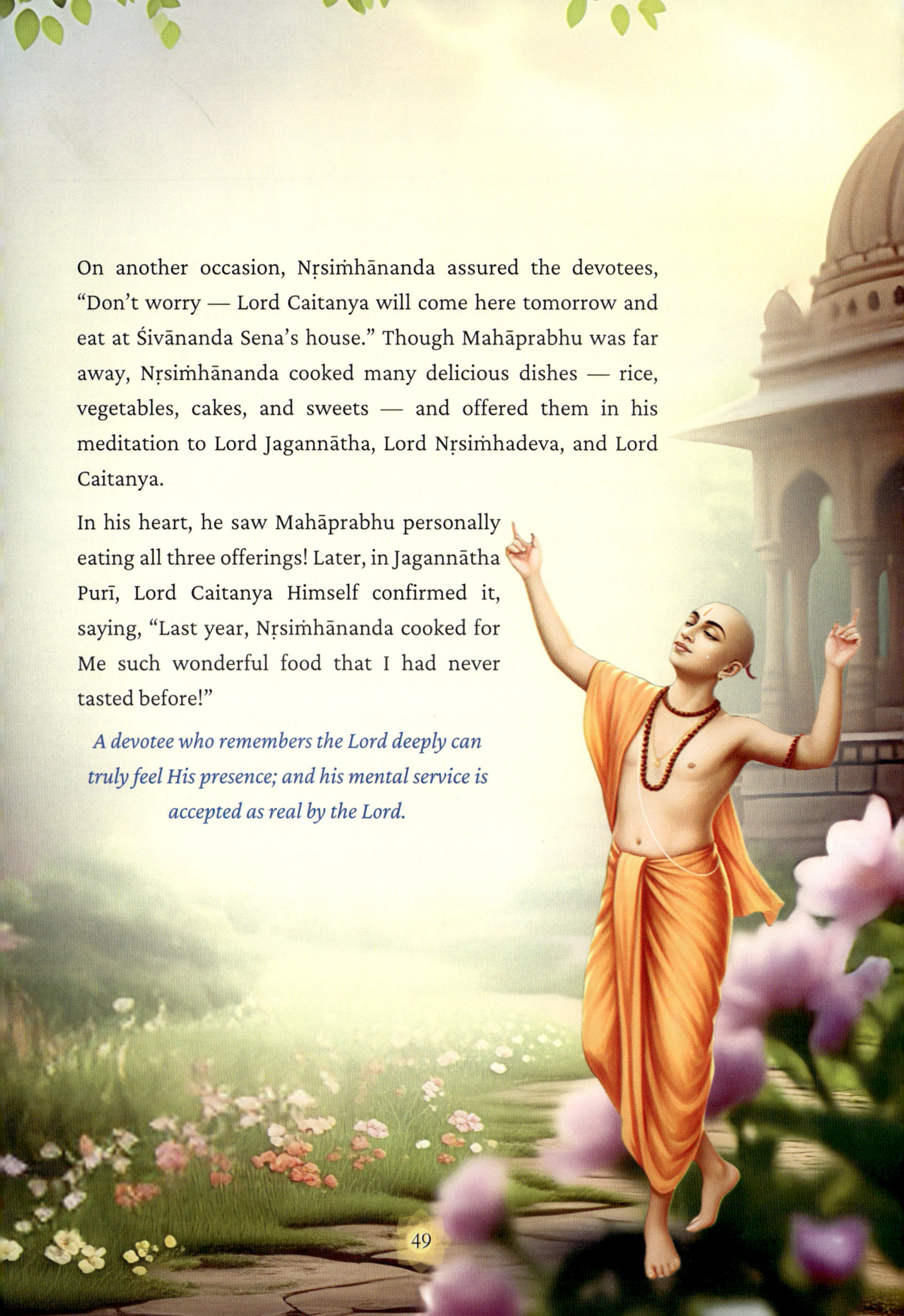

# Let's Remember!

*Smaraṇam* or remembering Kṛṣṇa is the essence of all rules and regulations of *bhakti*. Whether it was little Prahlāda in danger, Mother Sītā in sorrow, King Khaṭvāṅga in his last moment, or the Pāṇḍavas in all situations of life — remembrance gave them strength, protection, and joy. Lord Caitanya showed us how remembrance can overflow in love, and devotees like Narasimhananda *Brahmacārī* revealed how one can feel the personal presence of the Lord through smaraṇam.

Just as we always remember someone we love — a friend, a parent, or a favorite hero — a devotee keeps remembering Kṛṣṇa, the best friend of all living beings. That is the secret of spiritual happiness!

## Benefits of Smaraṇam

| | | |
|---|---|---|
| 1 | **Strength** | Gives courage in times of danger or fear. |
| 2 | **Hope** | Brings comfort in sorrow and loneliness. |
| 3 | **Love** | Deepens our bond of affection with Kṛṣṇa. |
| 4 | **Protection** | Invites Kṛṣṇa's shelter in helpless situations. |
| 5 | **Victory** | Helps us overcome life's challenges with grace. |

1
Begin your day by remembering Kṛṣṇa's name.

2
Keep a small picture or item of Kṛṣṇa nearby to remind you of Him during the day.

3
Whenever you feel worried, stop and softly remember a pastime of Kṛṣṇa.

4
Before sleeping, replay one story of Kṛṣṇa in your mind like a bedtime movie.

5
Whenever you receive something nice, remember it is Kṛṣṇa's gift.

SIMPLE WAYS TO PRACTICE SMARAṆAM

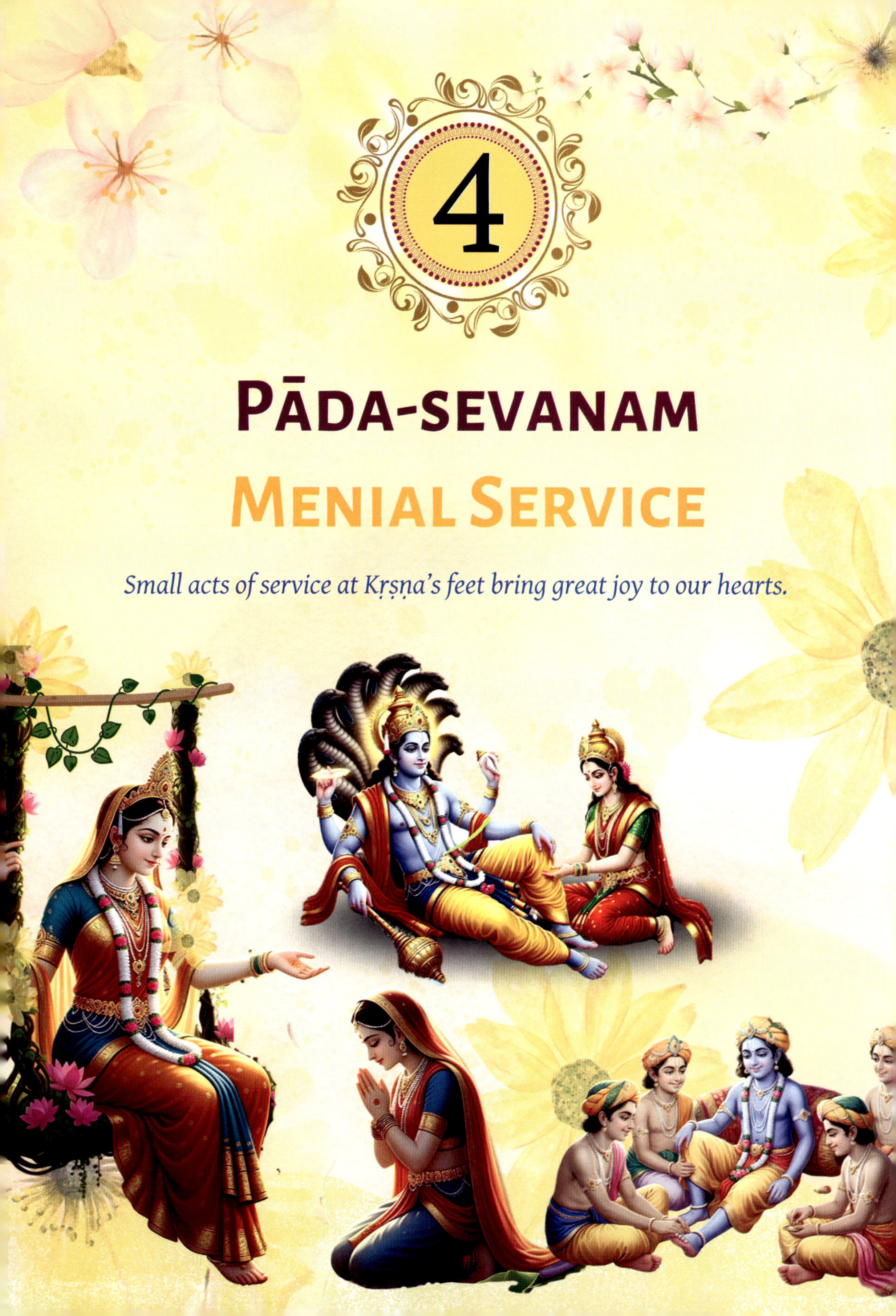
4

PĀDA-SEVANAM
MENIAL SERVICE

Small acts of service at Kṛṣṇa's feet bring great joy to our hearts.

*Pāda-sevanam* or remembrance of the Lord becomes perfect when we constantly meditate on the Lord's lotus feet and desire to serve them. In spiritual life, the feet of Kṛṣṇa are the place of shelter, surrender, and loving service. Service to the Lord begins at His feet — not head — to remind us of our small position in front of Him, and thus become humble. This is called *Pāda-sevanam* – rendering humble, menial services to the Lord's lotus feet, and everything that is connected to Him.

By engaging both our body and mind in such service, we quickly grow attached to the Lord and advance in devotion. Serving the Lord's lotus feet is like saying, "O Kṛṣṇa, I am Yours. Please keep me under the shelter of Your feet forever."

### SOME FORMS OF PĀDA-SEVANAM RECOMMENDED IN THE SCRIPTURES

| | | |
|---|---|---|
| 1 | **DARŚANA:** | Seeing the Lord's Deity form in the temple. |
| 2 | **SPARŚA:** | Touching the Deity's lotus feet or the dust of His temple. |
| 3 | **PARIKRAMĀ:** | Walking around His temple or holy *dhāma* in respect. |
| 4 | **TADĪYA-SEVĀ:** | Serving those dear to Him — the Vaiṣṇavas, Tulasī Devī, Gaṅgā & Yamunā. |
| 5 | **TĪRTHA-SEVĀ:** | Every *tīrtha* (holy place or river) lives at the Lord's feet. |

So we serve the Lord's lotus feet by bathing in Rivers Gaṅgā or Yamunā, which flow from His Lord's feet, and visiting holy places like Jagannātha Purī, Dvārakā, and Mathurā.

*Pāda-sevanam* also includes sweeping and decorating the temple, gathering flowers and fruits, carrying the Lord in joyous processions, offering tulasī leaves and water to His feet, or simply walking to His temple barefoot with love. Here are some shining examples of *Pāda-sevanam* done by exalted devotees from our scriptures.

# 1. Goddess Lakṣmī, the Eternal Servant of the Lord's Feet

Lakṣmī Devī, the goddess of fortune, is worshiped by kings, sages, and devatas for blessings of wealth and beauty. Yet, with all her opulence, she desires only one thing — to serve the lotus feet of Lord Nārāyaṇa. She always lovingly massages His feet, and bestows her real blessings upon her worshipers only if they worship Lord Narayana. If someone wants only Lakshmi and not Narayana, she is not impressed with such a worshiper. Mother Lakshmi not only serves Narayana's feet, but also sweeps the jewelled floors and the walls of Vaikuṇṭha, and eagerly waiting for His merciful glance. Her joy is not in being adored by others, but in staying forever at the Lord's feet as His servant.

*The goddess of fortune finds her joy at the Lord's feet — so should we.*

## 2. Kṛṣṇa's Queens – Humble Servants Despite Royalty

In Dvārakā, Kṛṣṇa lived with 16,108 queens. Each was a princess surrounded by wealth, jewels, and thousands of maidservants. Yet, instead of enjoying royal comforts, they personally cooked for Kṛṣṇa, served Him, and performed even simple chores with love. Rukmiṇī Devī, though she had countless attendants, served Kṛṣṇa herself, considering it her greatest honor.

Once, during a great gathering at *Kurukṣetra*, Draupadī met all of Kṛṣṇa's queens. Each narrated how she had married the Lord, but all expressed the same feeling: their greatest fortune was not being Kṛṣṇa's queens, but being His humble maidservants.

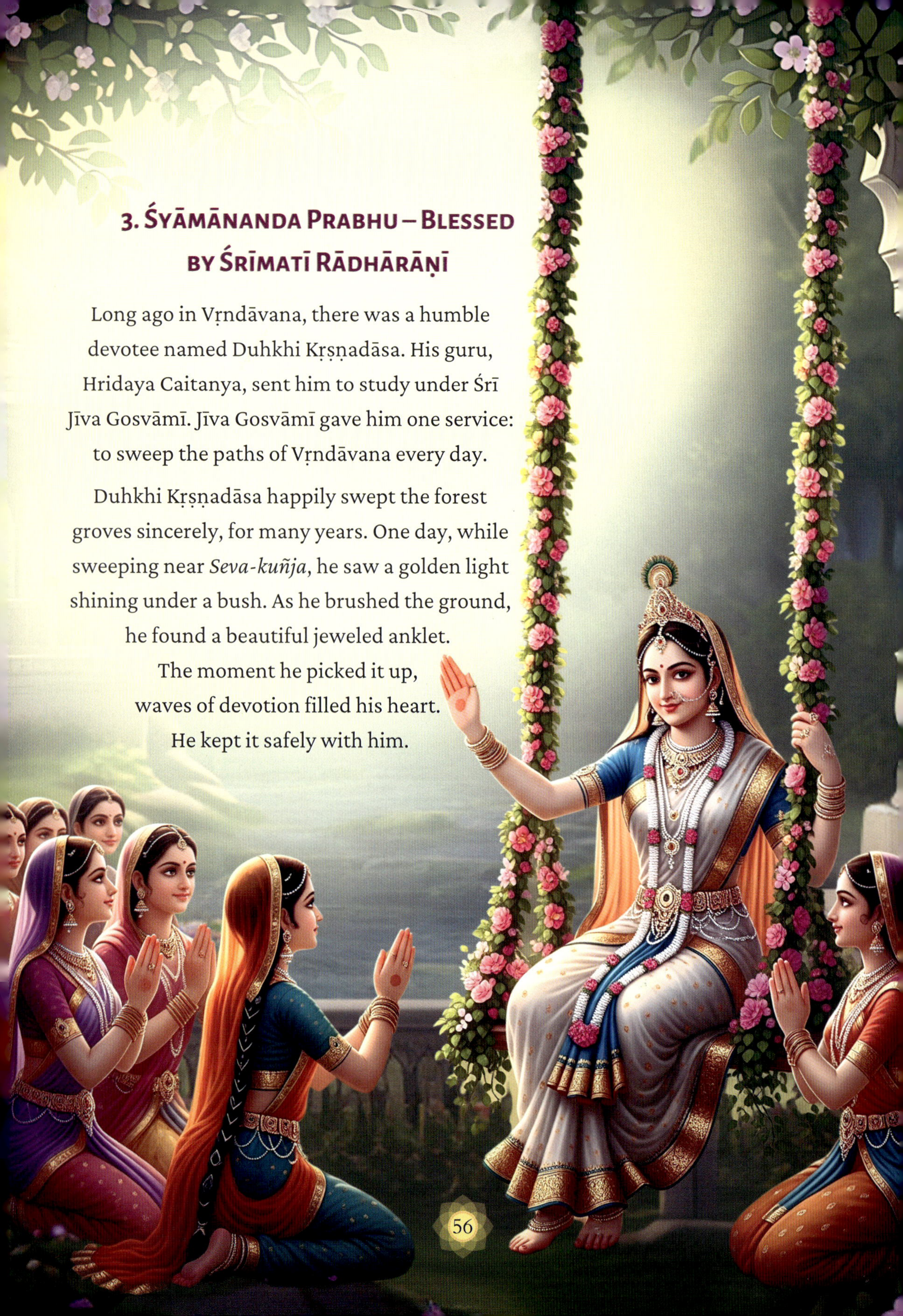

### 3. Śyāmānanda Prabhu – Blessed by Śrīmatī Rādhārāṇī

Long ago in Vṛndāvana, there was a humble devotee named Duhkhi Kṛṣṇadāsa. His guru, Hridaya Caitanya, sent him to study under Śrī Jīva Gosvāmī. Jīva Gosvāmī gave him one service: to sweep the paths of Vṛndāvana every day.

Duhkhi Kṛṣṇadāsa happily swept the forest groves sincerely, for many years. One day, while sweeping near *Seva-kuñja*, he saw a golden light shining under a bush. As he brushed the ground, he found a beautiful jeweled anklet. The moment he picked it up, waves of devotion filled his heart. He kept it safely with him.

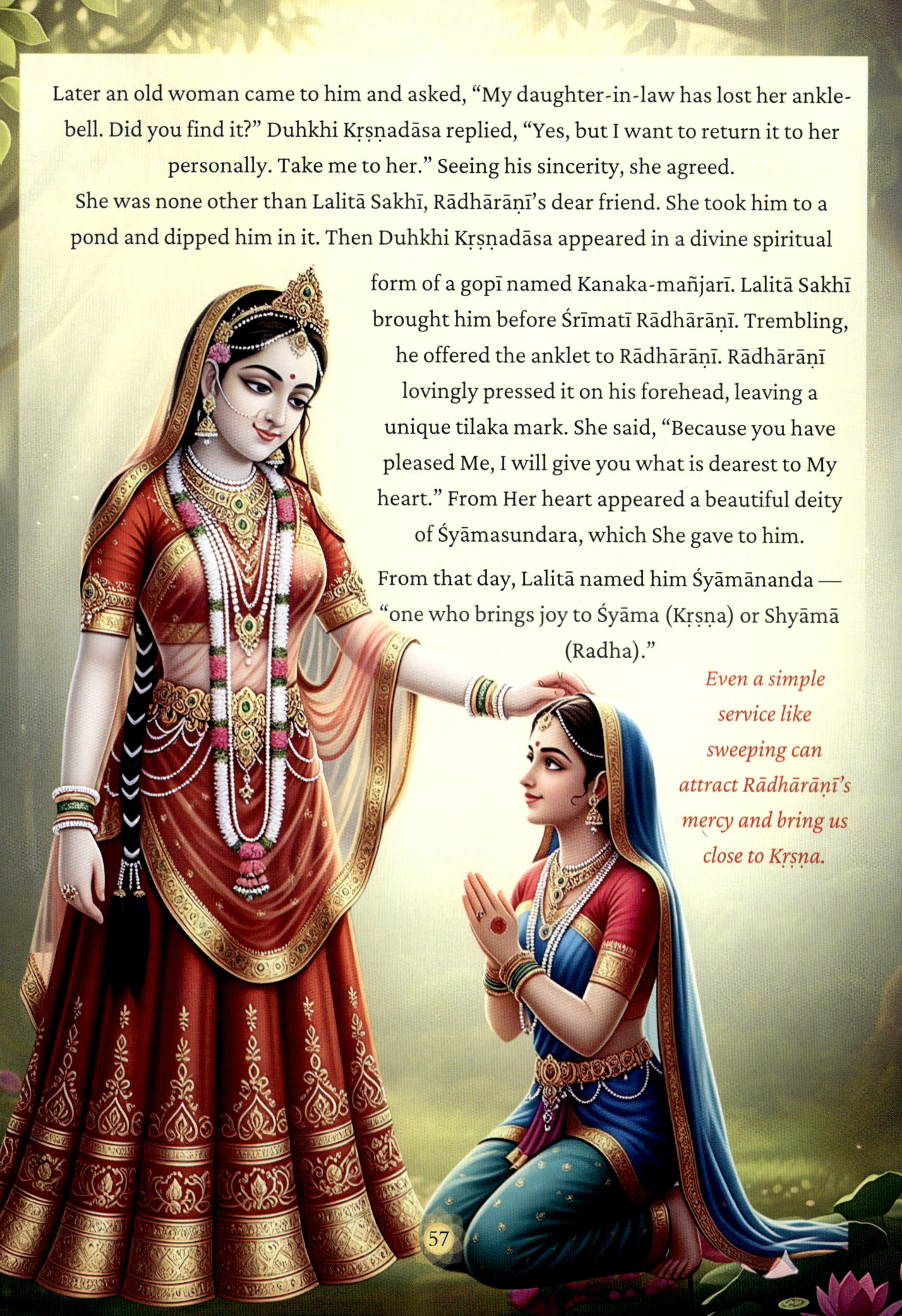

Later an old woman came to him and asked, "My daughter-in-law has lost her ankle-bell. Did you find it?" Duhkhi Kṛṣṇadāsa replied, "Yes, but I want to return it to her personally. Take me to her." Seeing his sincerity, she agreed.

She was none other than Lalitā Sakhī, Rādhārāṇī's dear friend. She took him to a pond and dipped him in it. Then Duhkhi Kṛṣṇadāsa appeared in a divine spiritual form of a gopī named Kanaka-mañjarī. Lalitā Sakhī brought him before Śrīmatī Rādhārāṇī. Trembling, he offered the anklet to Rādhārāṇī. Rādhārāṇī lovingly pressed it on his forehead, leaving a unique tilaka mark. She said, "Because you have pleased Me, I will give you what is dearest to My heart." From Her heart appeared a beautiful deity of Śyāmasundara, which She gave to him.

From that day, Lalitā named him Śyāmānanda — "one who brings joy to Śyāma (Kṛṣṇa) or Shyāmā (Radha)."

*Even a simple service like sweeping can attract Rādhārāṇī's mercy and bring us close to Kṛṣṇa.*

# 4. King Pratāparudra's Humility

King Pratāparudra ruled the wealthy kingdom of Orissa, but in his heart, he longed for only one treasure — the mercy of Lord Caitanya Mahāprabhu. Yet Mahāprabhu was strict about avoiding contact with worldly kings and refused to meet him. The king was heartbroken.

But his humility shone through. During the grand *Ratha-yātrā* festival, when Lord Jagannātha was taken out of His temple and placed on His chariot, King Pratāparudra took up a golden broom and swept the road before the Lord's cart. Though he was a mighty king, he felt no shame — he was simply glad to clean the path for the Lord's lotus feet. From a distance, Lord Caitanya saw this service and was deeply pleased.

Later, in the Jagannātha Vallabha gardens, Mahāprabhu was resting after hours of ecstatic dancing. The king came dressed not in royal clothes, but as a simple *Vaiṣṇava*. With great devotion, he began softly reciting the *Gopī-gīta*

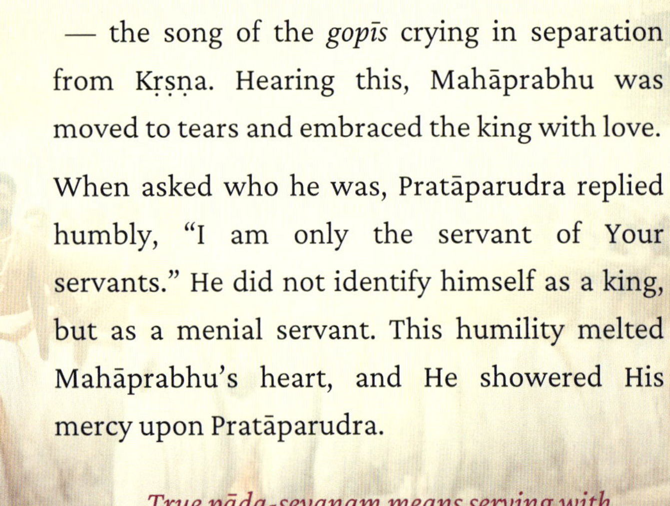

— the song of the *gopīs* crying in separation from Kṛṣṇa. Hearing this, Mahāprabhu was moved to tears and embraced the king with love.

When asked who he was, Pratāparudra replied humbly, "I am only the servant of Your servants." He did not identify himself as a king, but as a menial servant. This humility melted Mahāprabhu's heart, and He showered His mercy upon Pratāparudra.

*True pāda-sevanam means serving with humility — no matter what our position may be.*

# 5. Balarāma and the Gopas Massage Kṛṣṇa's Feet

In the forests of Vṛndāvana, little Kṛṣṇa and His brother Balarāma would spend long days playing with Their cowherd friends. They would run, wrestle, climb trees, herd the cows, and sometimes fight mock battles with sticks. After hours of such exciting play, Kṛṣṇa would sometimes feel tired and sit down beneath a shady tree.

Seeing Him resting, Balarāma and the *gopas* would immediately gather around with loving concern. Some fanned Him gently with leaves, some massaged His arms and shoulders, and others pressed His soft lotus feet. Balarāma especially delighted in serving His younger brother this way — sometimes massaging Kṛṣṇa's feet, sometimes even placing Kṛṣṇa's head on His lap and fanning Him with great affection.

And Kṛṣṇa accepted these simple, loving services with a smile. For Him, the hands of His friends touching His feet were sweeter than any royal comfort. For the *gopas,* the greatest joy of their play was not just winning games, but serving their beloved Kṛṣṇa.

*Devotees are attracted to the feet of the Lord just as honey bees are attracted to a lotus flower.*

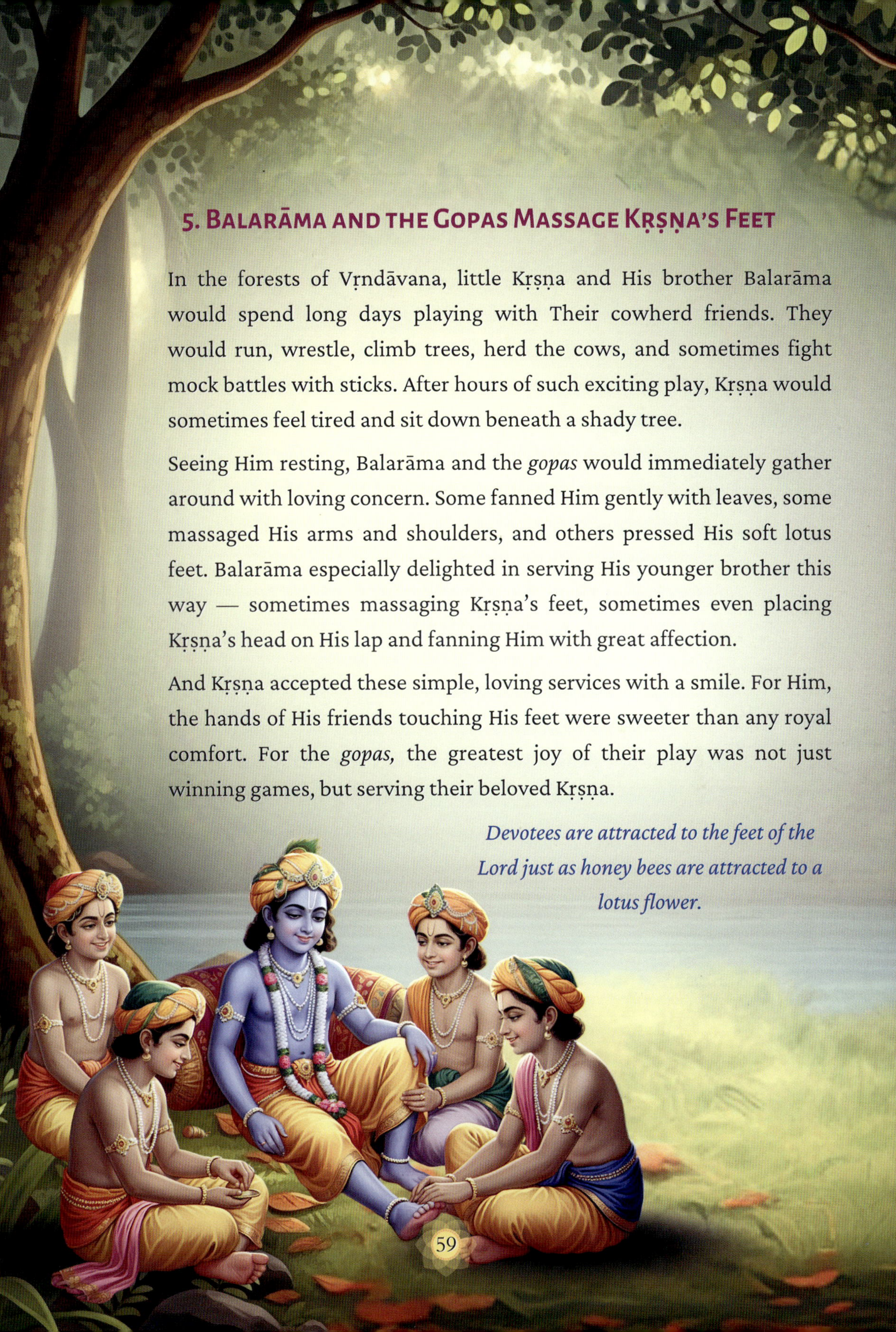

## Let's Serve!

*Pāda-sevanam* teaches us that true greatness lies in humble service. Whether it is Goddess Lakṣmī massaging Lord Nārāyaṇa's feet, queens like Rukmiṇī personally serving Kṛṣṇa, King Pratāparudra sweeping before Lord Jagannātha's chariot, Śyāmānanda Prabhu sweeping the paths of Vṛndāvana or the little gopas pressing Kṛṣṇa's feet — all these exalted devotees found their greatest joy at the Lord's lotus feet.

When we bend down to serve the Lord's feet, our hearts bend too — becoming soft, humble, and filled with love.

### BENEFITS OF PĀDA-SEVANAM

| | | |
|---|---|---|
| 1 | **Humility** | Reminds us of our small position and dependence on Kṛṣṇa. |
| 2 | **Connection** | Brings us under the Lord's personal shelter. |
| 3 | **Engagement** | Keeps our body and mind busy in meaningful service. |
| 4 | **Blessings** | Attracts the mercy of Kṛṣṇa and His devotees. |
| 5 | **Joy** | Fills the heart with satisfaction and peace. |

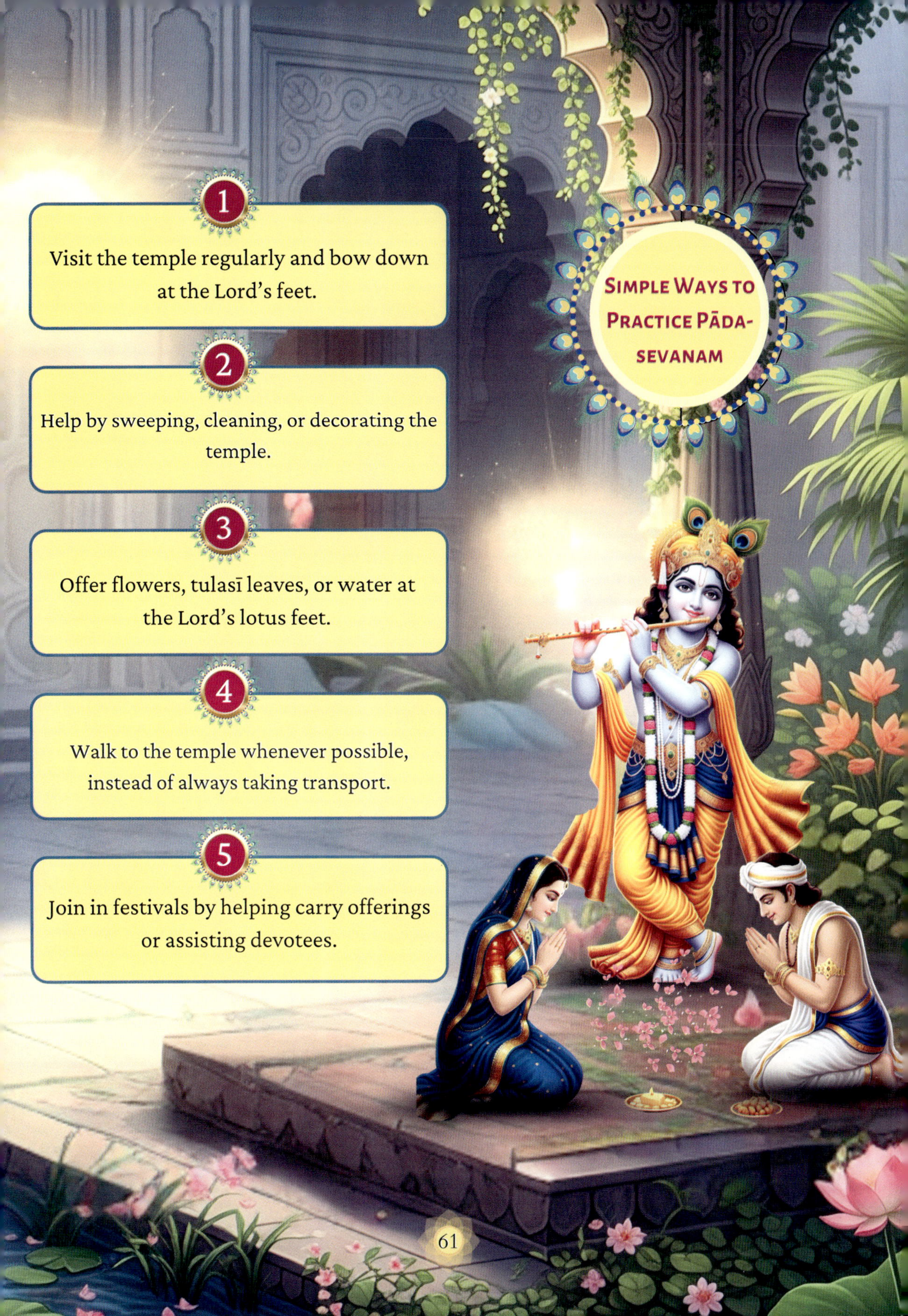

SIMPLE WAYS TO PRACTICE PĀDA-SEVANAM

1
Visit the temple regularly and bow down at the Lord's feet.

2
Help by sweeping, cleaning, or decorating the temple.

3
Offer flowers, tulasī leaves, or water at the Lord's lotus feet.

4
Walk to the temple whenever possible, instead of always taking transport.

5
Join in festivals by helping carry offerings or assisting devotees.

# 5

# ARCANAM

## WORSHIP

*To worship Kṛṣṇa is to declare that He is the center of our lives*

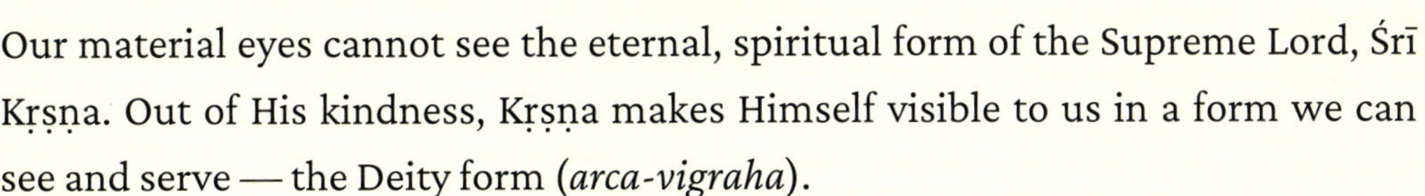

Our material eyes cannot see the eternal, spiritual form of the Supreme Lord, Śrī Kṛṣṇa. Out of His kindness, Kṛṣṇa makes Himself visible to us in a form we can see and serve — the Deity form (*arca-vigraha*).

Deities may be made of different materials — clay, stone, wood, metal, jewels, paint — or even worshiped within the mind. When carved according to scriptural descriptions and installed by devotees with proper rituals, the Deity is not different from Kṛṣṇa Himself. In this merciful form, the Lord personally manifests on the altar to receive our offerings, hear our prayers, and shower His blessings.

This process of worshiping the Lord in His Deity form is called arcanam, one of the nine important limbs of bhakti. Worship may involve many articles and rituals, but the most essential ingredient is devotion. Lord Kṛṣṇa Himself mentioned this in the Bhagavad-gītā (9.26):

*patraṁ puṣpaṁ phalaṁ toyaṁ yo me bhaktyā prayacchati*
*tad ahaṁ bhakty-upahṛtam aśnāmi prayatātmanaḥ*

"If one offers Me with love and devotion a leaf, a flower, fruit, or water, I will accept it."

Worship of the Lord does not depend on wealth or grandeur. Even the poorest person can please Kṛṣṇa if the offering is made with sincerity and love. A single tulasī leaf, a little water, or a simple flower offered with devotion delights Him. And if even these cannot be offered physically, then offerings made in the heart are kindly accepted by the Lord.

At the same time, when Kṛṣṇa blesses someone with wealth, that wealth should be used in His worship. Just as watering the root of a tree nourishes all its branches, worshiping the Lord in His Deity form nourishes the soul and brings benefit to all.



Uddhava glorified the power of honoring even the Lord's remnants:

*tvayopabhukta-srag-gandha-vāso-'laṅkāra-carcitāḥ*
*ucchiṣṭa-bhojino dāsās tava māyāṁ jayema hi*

"Simply by honoring the garlands, fragrances, clothes, and ornaments You have used, and by eating the remnants of Your meals, we, Your servants, can conquer Your illusory energy." (SB 11.6.46)

When worship is performed with devotion, it not only honors the Lord but also purifies our hearts.

*Arcanam* trains us to see everything as belonging to Kṛṣṇa and inspires us to offer back to Him the best of what we have. *Arcanam* helps us realize that we are not the body but soul.

Worship is not just ritual. It is an expression of love — saying, "Kṛṣṇa, everything I have is Yours. Please accept this humble offering."

Here are some beautiful stories of devotees who exemplified deity worship.

# 1. The Poor Brāhmaṇa's Mental Worship

In the city of Pratiṣṭhānapura lived a poor *brāhmaṇa* who longed to serve Lord Viṣṇu, but he had no wealth to perform elaborate Deity worship. One day, he heard in a discourse, "If you cannot afford to offer fine clothes, ornaments, or food to the Lord, you can still worship Him sincerely through meditation."

Inspired, the *brāhmaṇa* began daily mental worship. After bathing in the river, he would sit quietly and imagine in detail — dressing Lord Viṣṇu in silks and jewels, cleaning His temple, offering fragrant flowers, incense, fruits, and delicious dishes. He performed this worship in his mind with deep love, day after day, for many years.

One day, while meditating, he prepared sweet rice for the Lord. To test if it had cooled, he touched it— and to his amazement, his finger was burnt in real life!

At that very moment in Vaikuṇṭha, Lord Viṣṇu burst into laughter, delighted by His devotee's sincerity. Goddess Lakṣmī asked, "My Lord, what makes You laugh so joyfully?" The Lord told His attendants: "Go to Pratiṣṭhānapura and bring that brāhmaṇa here." The Lord's servants immediately brought the brāhmaṇa to Vaikuṇṭha in a celestial airplane. Lord Viṣṇu then narrated the entire story to Goddess Lakṣmī, praising the *brāhmaṇa's* unwavering devotion. As a reward for his heartfelt service, Lord Viṣṇu blessed him with eternal residence in Vaikuṇṭha.

*The Lord does not see the richness of our offerings —*
*He sees the richness of our love*

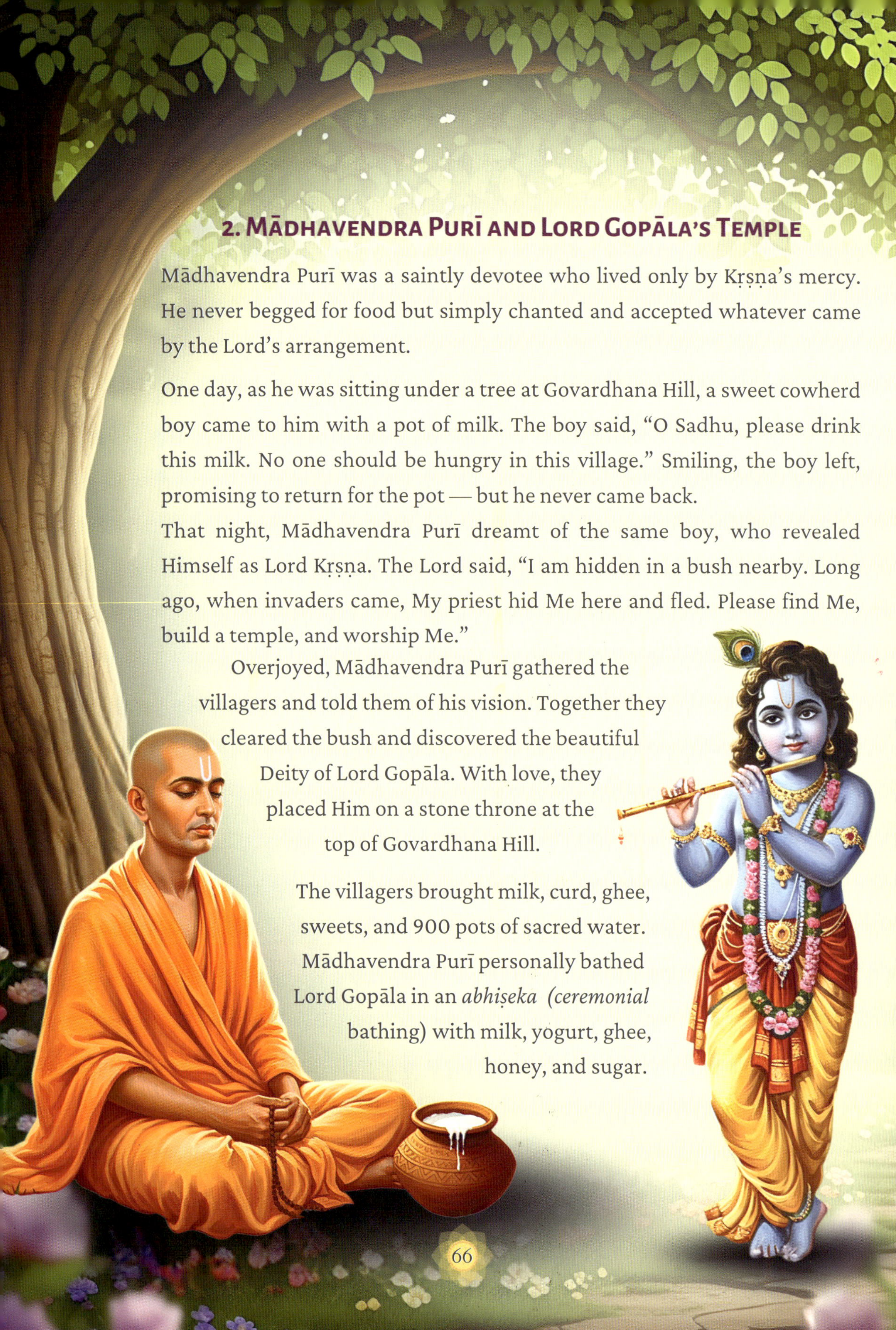

## 2. Mādhavendra Purī and Lord Gopāla's Temple

Mādhavendra Purī was a saintly devotee who lived only by Kṛṣṇa's mercy. He never begged for food but simply chanted and accepted whatever came by the Lord's arrangement.

One day, as he was sitting under a tree at Govardhana Hill, a sweet cowherd boy came to him with a pot of milk. The boy said, "O Sadhu, please drink this milk. No one should be hungry in this village." Smiling, the boy left, promising to return for the pot — but he never came back.

That night, Mādhavendra Purī dreamt of the same boy, who revealed Himself as Lord Kṛṣṇa. The Lord said, "I am hidden in a bush nearby. Long ago, when invaders came, My priest hid Me here and fled. Please find Me, build a temple, and worship Me."

Overjoyed, Mādhavendra Purī gathered the villagers and told them of his vision. Together they cleared the bush and discovered the beautiful Deity of Lord Gopāla. With love, they placed Him on a stone throne at the top of Govardhana Hill.

The villagers brought milk, curd, ghee, sweets, and 900 pots of sacred water. Mādhavendra Purī personally bathed Lord Gopāla in an *abhiṣeka (ceremonial bathing)* with milk, yogurt, ghee, honey, and sugar.

They dressed Him in fine garments, decorated Him with flowers, and offered mountains of food. The Lord, who had been hidden and unfed for many years, accepted everything and left *prasādam* for His devotees.

Soon, news of Gopāla's appearance spread everywhere. Devotees from nearby villages came daily with offerings.

Wealthy merchants from Mathurā brought gifts, and one rich man even built a beautiful temple.

What started as one saint's devotion became a grand festival of love, where all — rich and poor — worshiped Lord Gopāla together.

*Selfless service to the Lord completely satisfies the self.*

# 3. THE DEITY WHO STOLE THE OFFERINGS

Once Mādhavendra Purī visited a village called Remuṇā, where the beautiful Deity of Lord Gopīnātha was worshiped. There, he learned from the priest that the Lord was offered a special sweet called amṛta-keli.

Mādhavendra Purī thought, "If only I could taste this, I could prepare the same for my Gopāla in Vṛndāvana." But immediately he felt ashamed — "How can I desire the Lord's food before He eats it?" Feeling unworthy, he quietly left the temple and sat in the market, chanting the holy names.

That night, Lord Gopīnātha appeared in the dream of the priest and said, "I have hidden a pot of amṛta-keli behind Me. Take it and give it to My devotee, Mādhavendra Purī, who is chanting in the marketplace."

The humble priest awoke, bathed, and rushed to the altar. Behind the Deity he found the pot of sweet! Running to the market, he called out, "Mādhavendra Purī! The Lord has stolen this for you!"

The humble priest awoke, bathed, and rushed to the altar. Behind the Deity he found the pot of sweet! Running to the market, he called out, "Mādhavendra Purī! The Lord has stolen this for you!"

With tears of love, Mādhavendra Purī accepted the sweet, tasting it as Kṛṣṇa's mercy. He even kept the clay pot, and every day he would eat a little piece, feeling the Lord's love again and again.

From that day, Lord Gopīnātha became known as "Kṣīra-chor Gopīnātha" — the sweet-rice thief.

*The Deities in the temple reciprocate with a sincere devotee's desire.*

# 4. Anantācārya's Fearless Service

In the holy place of Tirupati lived Anantācārya, a disciple of Śrī Rāmānujācārya. He was known for his humble devotion and especially for cultivating fragrant flowers and tulasī leaves to offer daily to Lord Venkateśvara (Balaji).

One day, while working in the garden, Anantācārya was bitten by a venomous snake. But instead of panicking, he calmly continued plucking tulasī and preparing garlands. His disciples noticed it and rushed to him in fear and said, "Dear Gurudev! You must take medicine immediately! This snake's bite is deadly."

But Anantācārya only smiled and said, "I cannot interrupt my service to the Lord." The disciples, worried, went straight to Lord Venkateśvara and prayed desperately: "O Lord, please save our guru! He refuses treatment and may die!"

Hearing their prayer, Lord Venkateśvara spoke directly to Anantācārya: "My dear Ananta, you are bitten by a cobra. Please take medicine quickly. The poison is spreading in your body."

Anantācārya bowed his head and replied, "O Lord, which poison should I fear more? The poison of the snake, or the poison of pride, greed, anger, and ego within me? If the snake's poison is stronger than the poison within me, I will die.

Then I will bathe in the Virajā River at the gate of Vaikuṇṭha and serve You there. But if the poison within me is stronger than the snake's poison, I will survive. Then I will bathe in Swami Puṣkariṇī here and serve You at Tirumala. Either way, I remain Your servant." Lord Venkateśvara, delighted by his devotional mood, blessed him. Anantācārya survived the bite and continued serving the Lord with garlands.



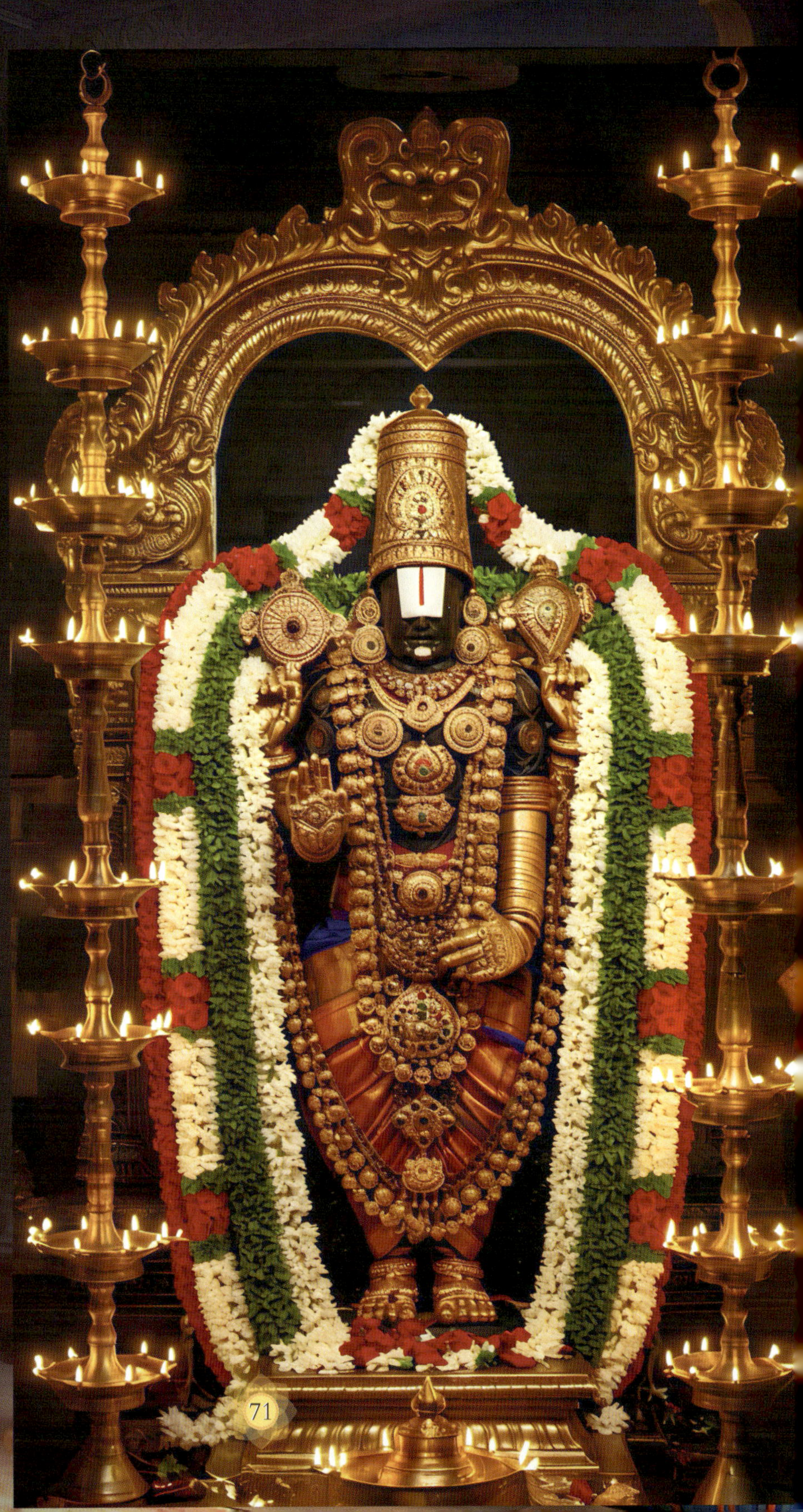

# 5. Raghunandan Feeds Lord Gopīnātha

Raghunandan was the young son of Mukunda, a great devotee of Lord Kṛṣṇa. Even at the tender age of five, he had a heart overflowing with devotion.

One day, Mukunda had to travel for some urgent work. Before leaving, he called his little son and said, "My dear child, our family has worshiped Lord Gopīnātha for generations. Today, you must feed Him. Just as your mother feeds us every day, you should feed Gopīnātha."

Eager to obey, Raghunandan collected all the items from his mother and entered the Deity room. He had often watched his father perform the rituals, so he carefully followed every step. Closing the curtain, ringing the bell, and chanting mantras, he placed the plate of food before the Lord. But after some time, the food remained untouched.

The boy's tender heart trembled. "Oh no! Father told me to feed the Lord, but He is not eating. What shall I do?" Tears rolled down his cheeks as he pleaded, "O Gopinātha, please eat! If You don't, Father will be upset."

Moved by his innocence, Lord Gopinātha smiled and said, "My child, I eat simply by glancing. Now this food is *prasādam* for you and your family."

But Raghunandan shook his head, insisting, "No, You must eat it with Your own hands!" Seeing the boy's determination, the Lord reached out and ate everything on the plate, leaving nothing behind. Raghunandan became very happy.

When Mukunda returned, he asked for *prasādam*. Raghunandan replied, "Father, Gopinātha ate it all — there is nothing left." Mukunda was astonished but knew his son was truthful. To test him further, he gave Raghunandan a laddu and asked him to offer it to the Deity. Hiding nearby, Mukunda watched in amazement as Gopinātha stretched out His hand, took the laddu, and ate half of it. With tears of joy, Mukunda embraced his son, realizing the Lord had accepted the love of his child.

*The attitude behind worship is more important than the magnitude of offerings.*

Once, Śrī Gopāla Bhaṭṭa Gosvāmī went to Nepal and bathed in the sacred Kālī-Gaṇḍakī River. As he dipped his waterpot into the river, something very unusual happened — many small black stones called Śālagrāma Śilās slipped inside his pot! He poured them back into the river, but when he refilled his pot, the Śilās came back again. This happened three times! Finally, he found twelve Śālagrāma

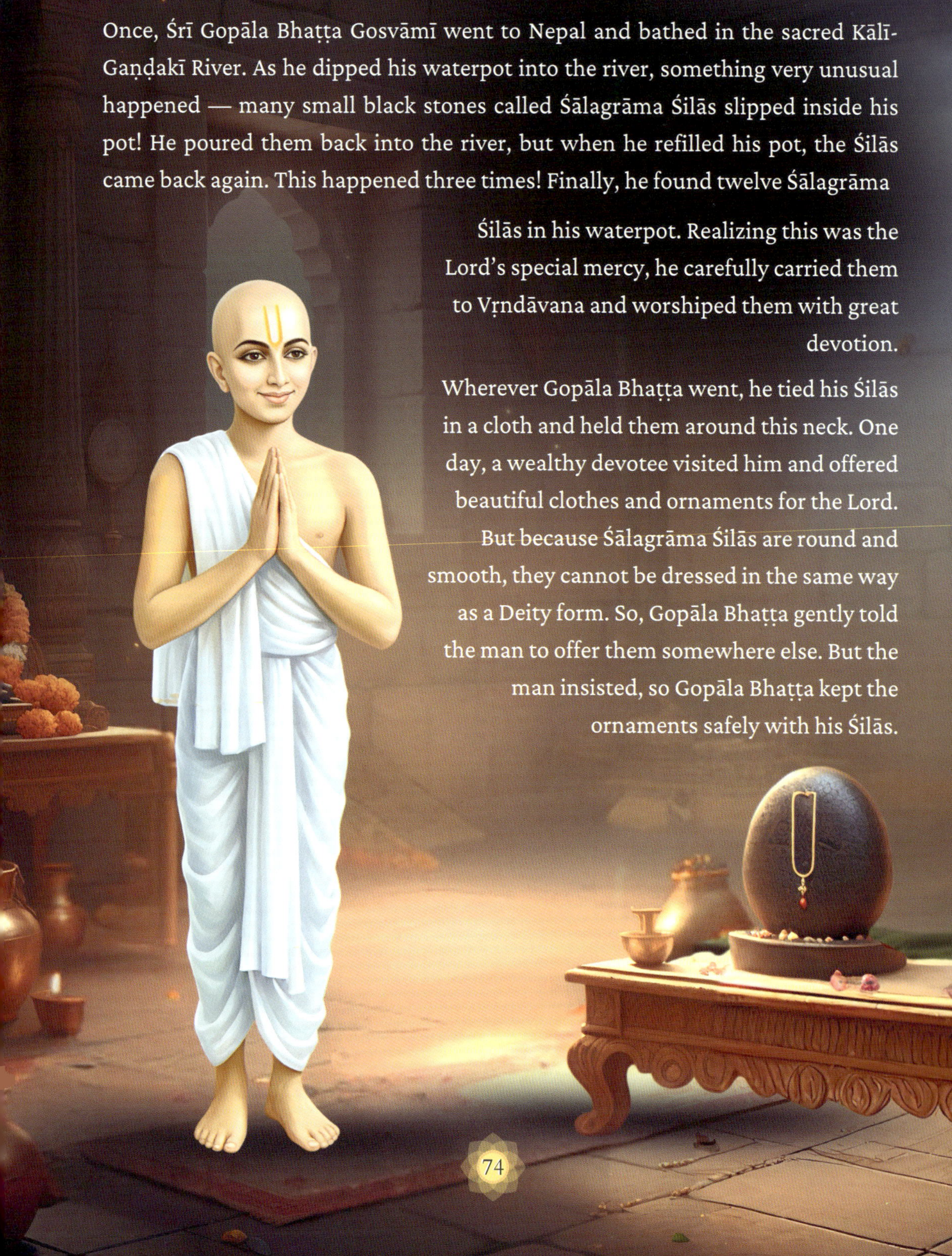

Śilās in his waterpot. Realizing this was the Lord's special mercy, he carefully carried them to Vṛndāvana and worshiped them with great devotion.

Wherever Gopāla Bhaṭṭa went, he tied his Śilās in a cloth and held them around this neck. One day, a wealthy devotee visited him and offered beautiful clothes and ornaments for the Lord. But because Śālagrāma Śilās are round and smooth, they cannot be dressed in the same way as a Deity form. So, Gopāla Bhaṭṭa gently told the man to offer them somewhere else. But the man insisted, so Gopāla Bhaṭṭa kept the ornaments safely with his Śilās.

That night, Gopāla Bhaṭṭa prayed. "My dear Lord, You are so kind. You always fulfill the wishes of Your devotees. If only I could serve You in a form with arms, legs, and a smiling face! Then I could lovingly dress You in these clothes and ornaments."

After offering bhoga and ārati, Gopāla Bhaṭṭa put his Śilās to rest and went to sleep. Early next morning, after bathing in the Yamunā, he came back to worship them. But he saw something astonishing! He could not believe his eyes! One of his Śālagrāma Śilās, the "Dāmodara Śilā," had transformed into a most beautiful Deity of Kṛṣṇa, standing in His three-fold bending form, playing the flute!

Gopāla Bhaṭṭa Gosvāmī was overwhelmed with joy and fell flat on the ground, offering prayers with tears in his eyes. Thus appeared Śrī Śrī Rādhā-Ramaṇa, one of the most enchanting and special Deities in Vṛndāvana.

*The deities reciprocate with the sincere desires of a dedicated worshiper.*

# Let's Worship!

*Arcanam* teaches us that worship is not about grandeur, but about love. Whether it was Mādhavendra Purī installing Lord Gopāla, Gopīnātha stealing sweet rice, young Raghunandan feeding the Lord with childlike faith, Anantācārya offering fearless service, or the poor *brāhmaṇa* worshiping in meditation — the Lord responded not to wealth or ritual, but to devotion.

Anyone, in any place, with any means, can worship the Lord. What matters is the sincerity of the heart. Worship means telling Kṛṣṇa: "Everything I have is Yours. Please accept my love."

## Benefits of Worshiping the Lord

| # | | |
|---|---|---|
| 1 | **Purification** | Cleanses the heart of fear, anger, envy, and pride. |
| 2 | **Connection** | Brings us close to Kṛṣṇa, who reciprocates with love. |
| 3 | **Protection** | The Lord protects His devotees who serve Him sincerely. |
| 4 | **Joy** | Worship fills life with peace, purpose, and happiness. |
| 5 | **Unity** | Brings families & communities together in service to the Lord. |
| 6 | **Grace** | Even small offerings attract the Lord's blessings. |
| 7 | **Eternal Gain** | Leads the soul to eternal service in Vaikuṇṭha. |

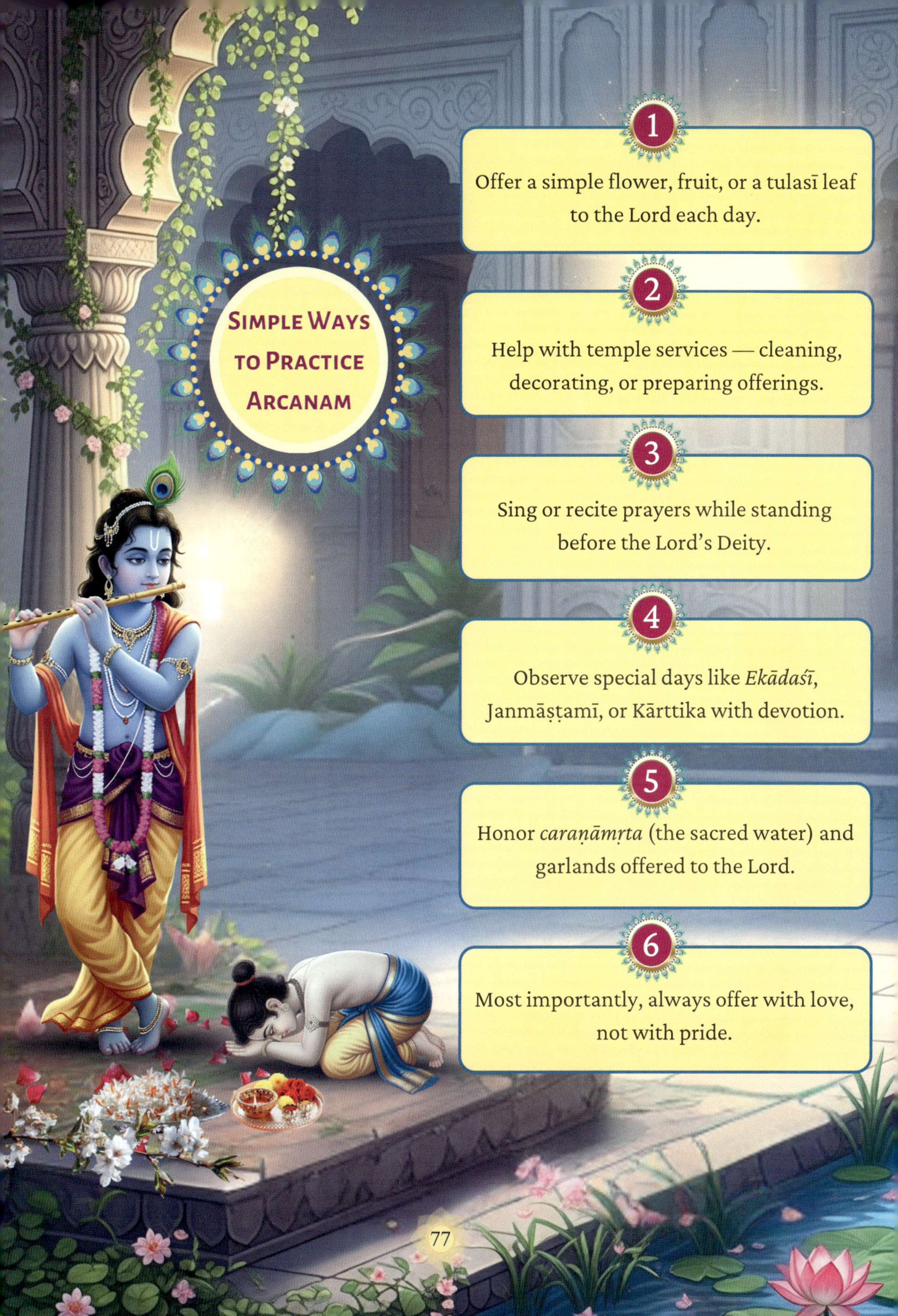

Simple Ways to Practice Arcanam

1
Offer a simple flower, fruit, or a tulasī leaf to the Lord each day.

2
Help with temple services — cleaning, decorating, or preparing offerings.

3
Sing or recite prayers while standing before the Lord's Deity.

4
Observe special days like Ekādaśī, Janmāṣṭamī, or Kārttika with devotion.

5
Honor caraṇāmṛta (the sacred water) and garlands offered to the Lord.

6
Most importantly, always offer with love, not with pride.

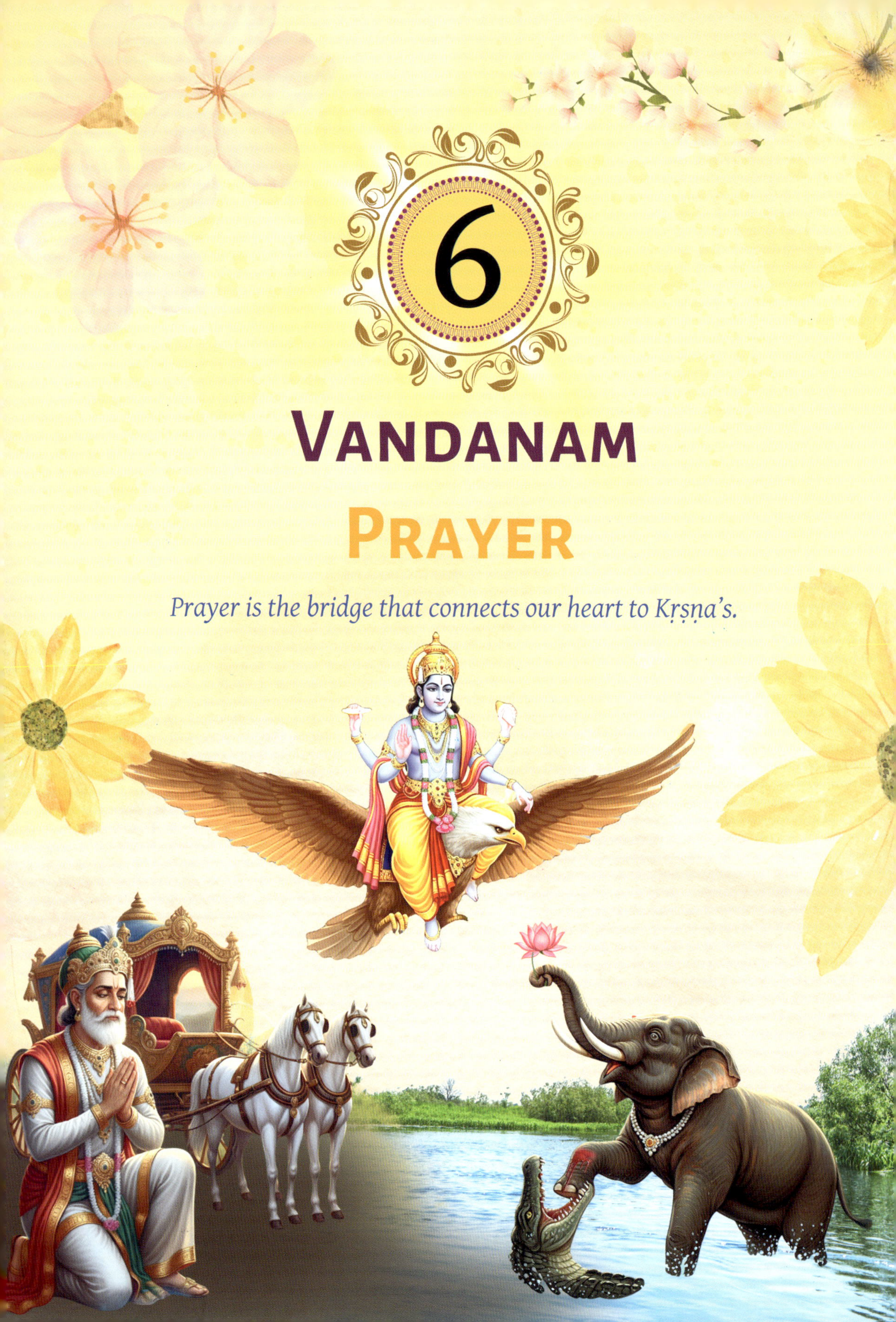

# 6

# Vandanam

## Prayer

*Prayer is the bridge that connects our heart to Kṛṣṇa's.*

*Arcanam* or worship of the Lord shouldn't simply be an external ritualistic act. Rather, it should be accompanied with an internal mood of prayer and devotion. If you ever write an empty letter to your friend do you think it will please them? No! It needs to have a heartfelt message written within. Similarly, our worship will bear complete fruit only when it is accompanied by our feelings and devotion. That's exactly what the next limb of bhakti talks about.

*Vandanam* means offering obeisances to the Lord with body, mind, and words.

| BODY | MIND | WORDS - PRAY, OFFER |
|------|------|---------------------|
| FOLD HANDS OR BOW DOWN. | STAY HUMBLE AND HONEST. | PRAISE, BEG FORGIVENESS AND EXPRESS LONGING |

The scriptures talk about three interesting moods
in which verbal prayers can be offered:

| ATTRACTION (SAMPRĀRTHANĀTMIKĀ) | HUMILITY (DAINYA-BODHIKĀ) | LONGING (LĀLASĀMAYĪ) |
|------|------|------|
| Dear Lord, may my mind be naturally drawn to You, like a flower to the sun, or iron particles to a magnet." | "O Lord, I have made mistakes. I feel ashamed. Please forgive me." | "O Lord, when will I get the chance to serve You closely, with love and tears in my eyes?" |

Prayers can be spoken, sung, whispered, or even said silently in the heart. What matters most is not the style, but the sincerity. A true prayer is simple and heartfelt — like a child speaking to a loving parent or a trusted friend.

Anyone can pray — young or old, rich or poor. Some devotees speak long, poetic prayers, while others simply say, "Thank You, Kṛṣṇa." Both are equally pleasing if spoken with sincerity.

Prayers remind us that Krishna is the Master and we are His children. It softens our pride and fills our heart with peace.

But what is the best prayer to make? Generally, many people in this world pray to fulfil their own wants and desires. However, the best prayers are about satisfying Kṛṣṇa. What Kṛṣṇa values most is not how long or fancy the prayer is, but that it comes straight from a loving and sincere heart.

Here are some wonderful examples of prayers offered by sincere devotees.

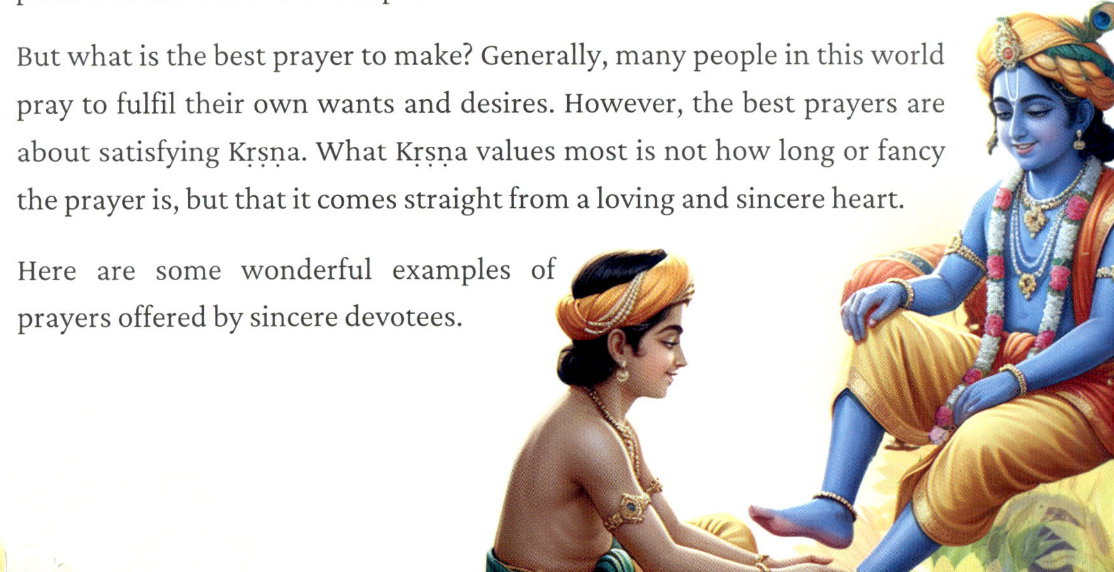

# 1. Mother Kunti's Prayer of Gratitude

After the great Kurukṣetra war, Queen Kuntī, the mother of the Pāṇḍavas, approached Kṛṣṇa with folded hands. She remembered how Kṛṣṇa had always protected her family — from a burning palace, from man-eating demons, from powerful weapons and enemies, and even from difficulties in the forest.

She prayed: "O Lord, again and again we faced dangers, and every time You appeared to save us I wish that all those calamities would happen again and again so that we could see You again and again, for seeing You means that we will no longer see repeated births and deaths."

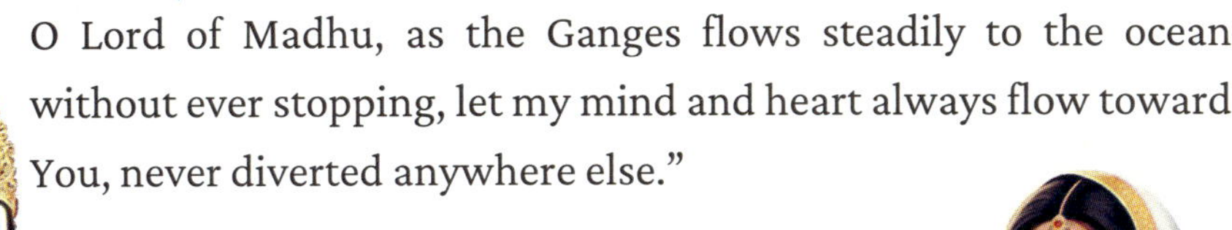

O Lord of Madhu, as the Ganges flows steadily to the ocean without ever stopping, let my mind and heart always flow toward You, never diverted anywhere else."

Most people pray for difficulties to end. But Kuntī prayed differently. She valued the remembrance of Kṛṣṇa so deeply that she was willing to face hardships if it meant never forgetting Him.

Kuntī's prayer shows us that real safety does not come from just avoiding problems but from remembering Kṛṣṇa always. When He is in our heart, no trouble can overcome us.

*Real safety is not the absence of problems, but the presence of Kṛṣṇa in our heart.*

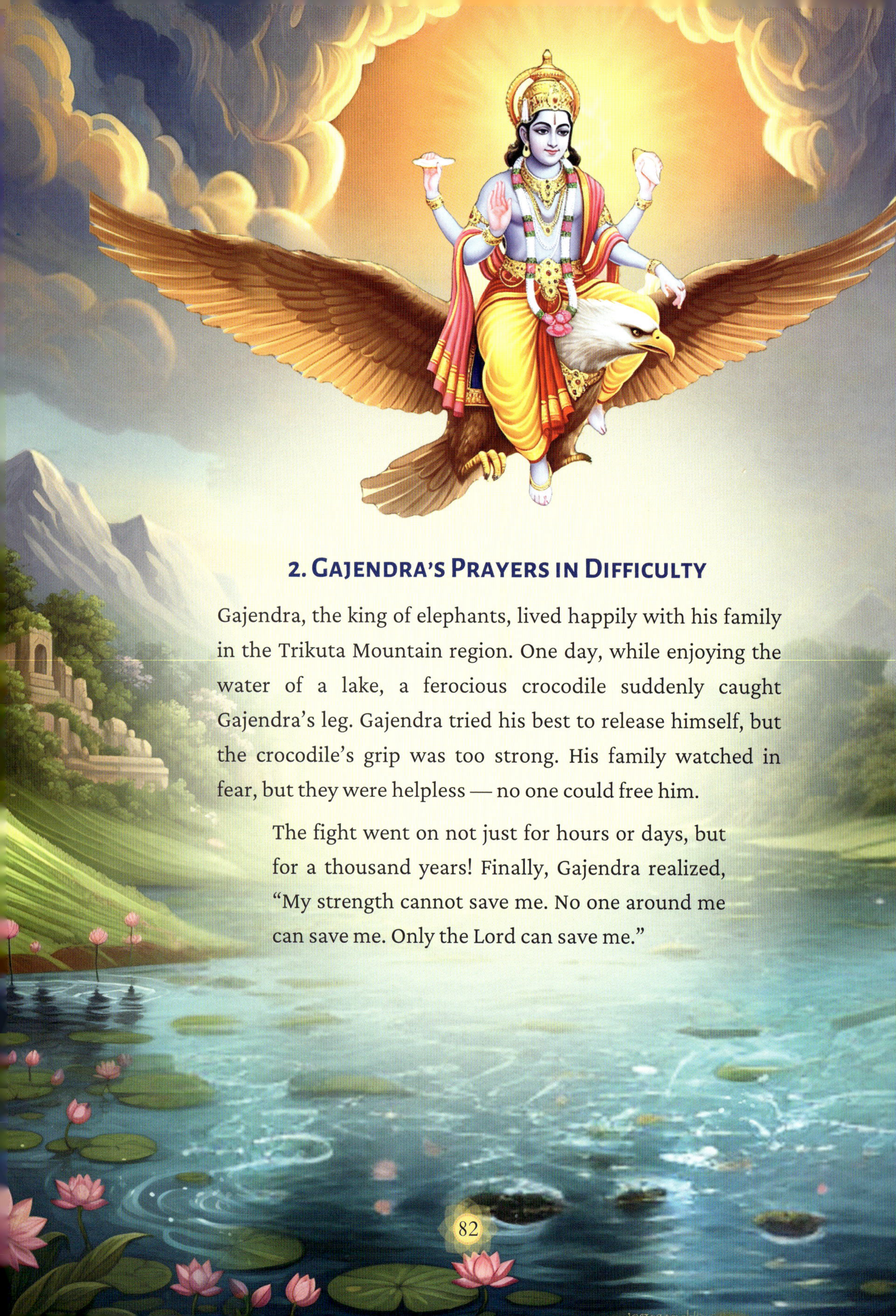

## 2. Gajendra's Prayers in Difficulty

Gajendra, the king of elephants, lived happily with his family in the Trikuta Mountain region. One day, while enjoying the water of a lake, a ferocious crocodile suddenly caught Gajendra's leg. Gajendra tried his best to release himself, but the crocodile's grip was too strong. His family watched in fear, but they were helpless — no one could free him.

The fight went on not just for hours or days, but for a thousand years! Finally, Gajendra realized, "My strength cannot save me. No one around me can save me. Only the Lord can save me."

By the Lord's grace, Gajendra then remembered a prayer he learnt in his past life. He said, "O Lord, You are the Supreme Father, the one who lives in everyone's heart. You are the master of all, the cause of everything, and the most merciful. Please save me! Being present in the hearts of all living beings, You are fully aware of their situation, and You are the only one who has the intention and ability to protect them if they surrender unto You. So, kindly save me from this calamity. I surrender completely at Your lotus feet."

Hearing this pure, desperate call, Lord Viṣṇu immediately came riding on Garuḍa, His eagle carrier. Seeing him, with great effort, Gajendra plucked a lotus flower from the lake, lifted it high with his trunk, and offered it to the Lord. In an instant, the Lord released His Sudarśana chakra and cut off the crocodile's head, freeing His dear devotee, Gajendra.

*Strength may fail, but prayer never fails —*
*the Lord always hears a sincere call from the heart.*

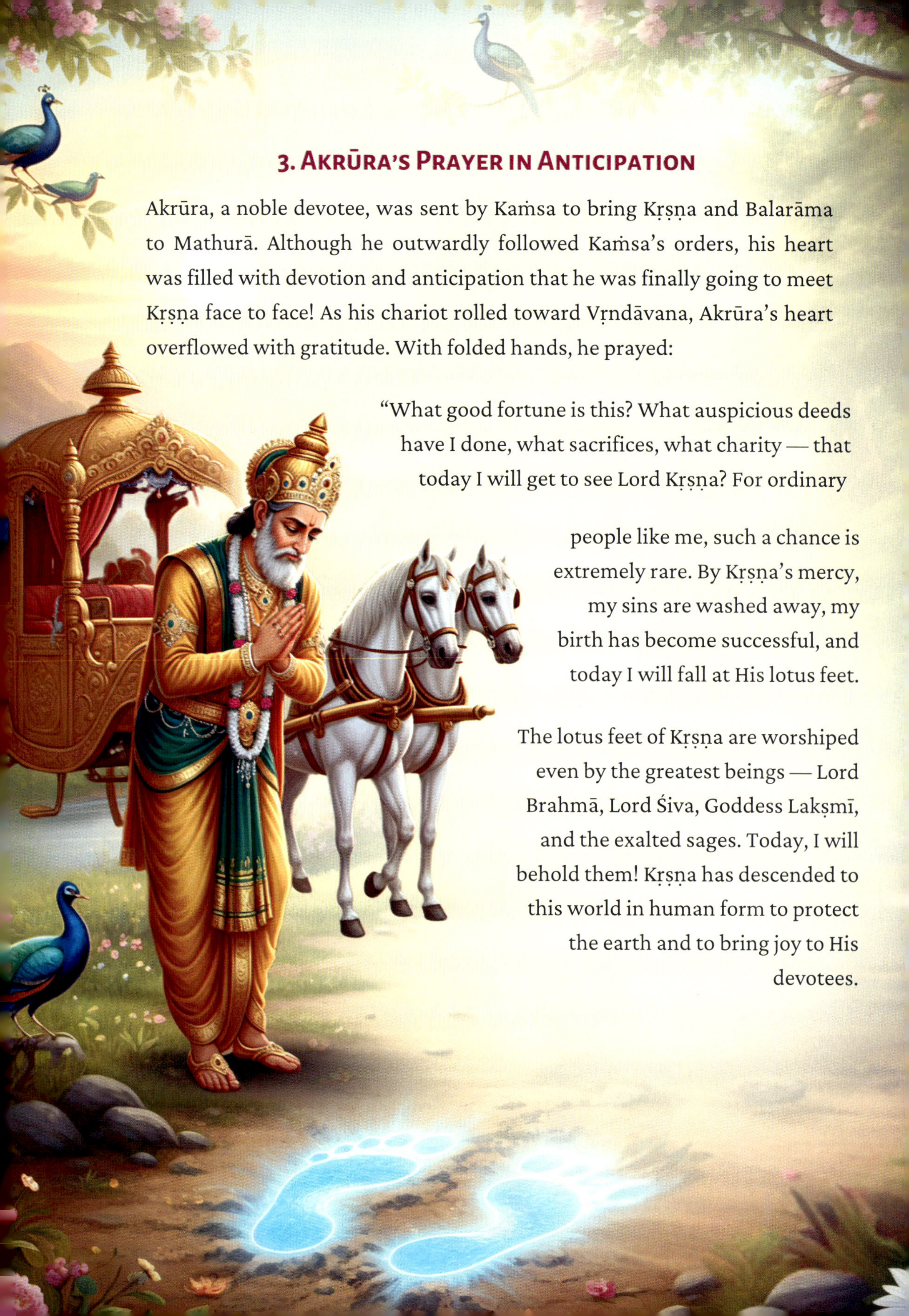

### 3. Akrūra's Prayer in Anticipation

Akrūra, a noble devotee, was sent by Kaṁsa to bring Kṛṣṇa and Balarāma to Mathurā. Although he outwardly followed Kaṁsa's orders, his heart was filled with devotion and anticipation that he was finally going to meet Kṛṣṇa face to face! As his chariot rolled toward Vṛndāvana, Akrūra's heart overflowed with gratitude. With folded hands, he prayed:

"What good fortune is this? What auspicious deeds have I done, what sacrifices, what charity — that today I will get to see Lord Kṛṣṇa? For ordinary people like me, such a chance is extremely rare. By Kṛṣṇa's mercy, my sins are washed away, my birth has become successful, and today I will fall at His lotus feet.

The lotus feet of Kṛṣṇa are worshiped even by the greatest beings — Lord Brahmā, Lord Śiva, Goddess Lakṣmī, and the exalted sages. Today, I will behold them! Kṛṣṇa has descended to this world in human form to protect the earth and to bring joy to His devotees.

Simply remembering His qualities and pastimes fills me with bliss. He is the reservoir of all beauty, the source of all good fortune, the destroyer of all suffering."

Akrūra imagined that when he reached Vṛndāvana, Kṛṣṇa would look at him with a sweet smile, place His lotus hand on his head, remove all his fears, and even address him affectionately: "My dear uncle Akrūra!" Thinking this, tears filled his eyes.

As his chariot entered the land of Vraja, Akrūra noticed the soft dust decorated with the footprints of Kṛṣṇa — marked with symbols of a lotus, a thunderbolt, a flag, and an elephant goad. Overcome with devotion, Akrūra descended from his chariot, offered obeisances to Kṛṣṇa's footprints, and rolled in the dust, saying, "Ah! Here are the footprints of my Master! This is the true goal of life — to leave aside pride, fear, and lamentation, and to absorb oneself in seeing, hearing, and glorifying all that reminds us of Kṛṣṇa."

Thus, even before meeting Kṛṣṇa, Akrūra's heart was bathing in prayers and remembrance. His Vandanam turned his journey into a festival of devotion.

*A prayerful journey to a holy place makes
the pilgrimage experience deeply spiritual.*

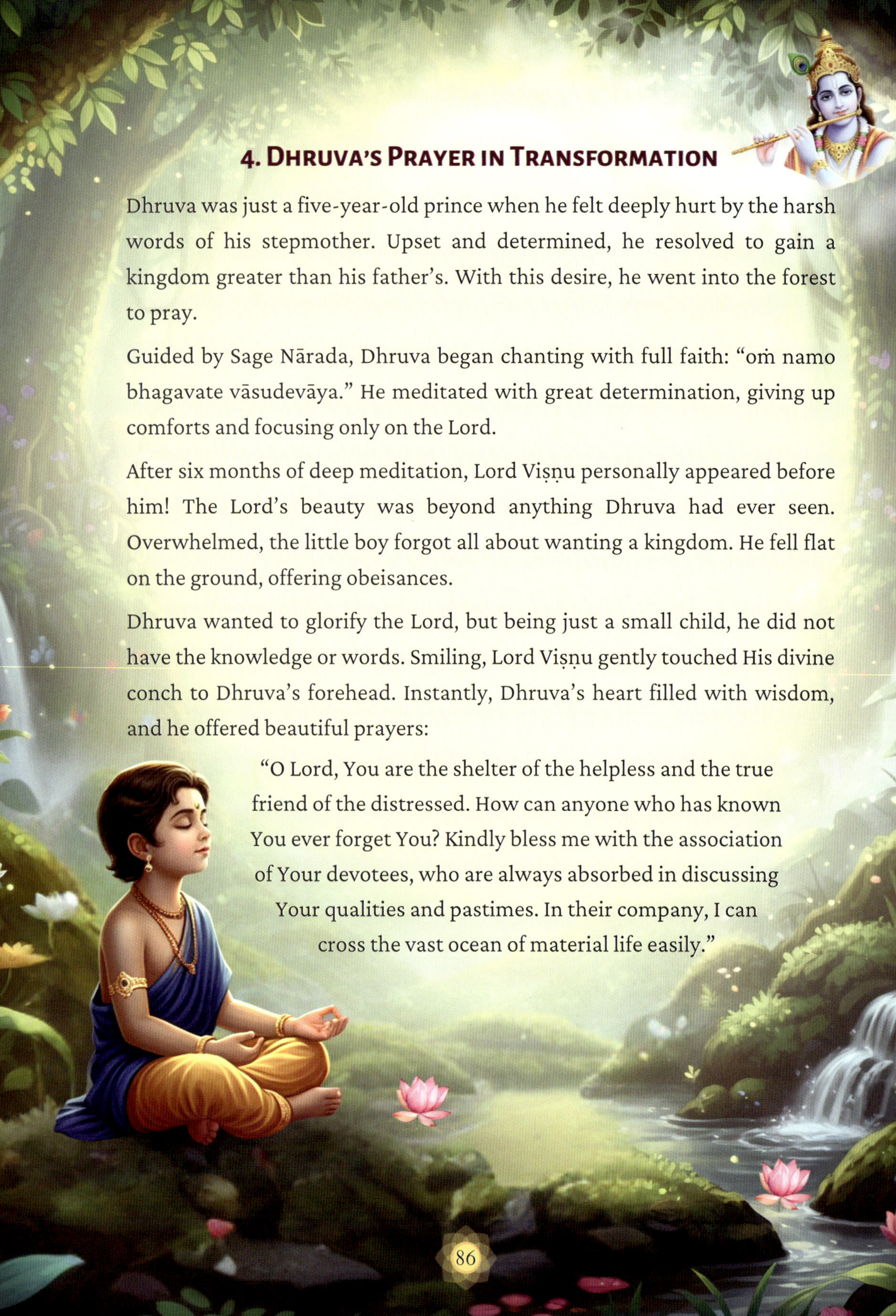

# 4. Dhruva's Prayer in Transformation

Dhruva was just a five-year-old prince when he felt deeply hurt by the harsh words of his stepmother. Upset and determined, he resolved to gain a kingdom greater than his father's. With this desire, he went into the forest to pray.

Guided by Sage Nārada, Dhruva began chanting with full faith: "oṁ namo bhagavate vāsudevāya." He meditated with great determination, giving up comforts and focusing only on the Lord.

After six months of deep meditation, Lord Viṣṇu personally appeared before him! The Lord's beauty was beyond anything Dhruva had ever seen. Overwhelmed, the little boy forgot all about wanting a kingdom. He fell flat on the ground, offering obeisances.

Dhruva wanted to glorify the Lord, but being just a small child, he did not have the knowledge or words. Smiling, Lord Viṣṇu gently touched His divine conch to Dhruva's forehead. Instantly, Dhruva's heart filled with wisdom, and he offered beautiful prayers:

"O Lord, You are the shelter of the helpless and the true friend of the distressed. How can anyone who has known You ever forget You? Kindly bless me with the association of Your devotees, who are always absorbed in discussing Your qualities and pastimes. In their company, I can cross the vast ocean of material life easily."

Dhruva then thought: "O Lord, I came seeking broken pieces of glass, but I have found a priceless jewel — You! I no longer want anything material. Please bless me to serve You always."

Though Dhruva had first approached the Lord with a material desire, the vision and mercy of Kṛṣṇa transformed his heart. He realized that love and service to the Lord is the greatest treasure of all.

*Hearing about the Lord in the association of devotees is the highest aspiration of a devotee.*

# 5. Prahlāda's Prayer of Compassion

After Lord Narasiṁhadeva killed the demon Hiraṇyakaśipu, little Prahlāda prayed sincerely with folded hands and a heart overflowing with humility:

"O Lord Nṛsiṁhadeva, Your appearance in this world brings protection, prosperity, and fearlessness to everyone. People will forever remember Your powerful form of Nṛsiṁha as their source of freedom from fear. I am not afraid of Your sharp teeth, fiery eyes, or roaring voice. What truly frightens me is the endless suffering of material life. This world is full of miseries and false hopes. Often, the so-called cures for suffering only make life even more painful! That is why I seek only Your shelter.

I will follow in the footsteps of the great sages and chant Your glories always. By remembering You, I have no fear. But I feel pain when I think of those who have turned away from You — people who only chase material pleasures and suffer again and again in the cycle of birth and death. O Lord, I do not wish to be saved alone. I pray for those foolish souls who are wandering blindly without knowing You. For them, I see no shelter other than You."

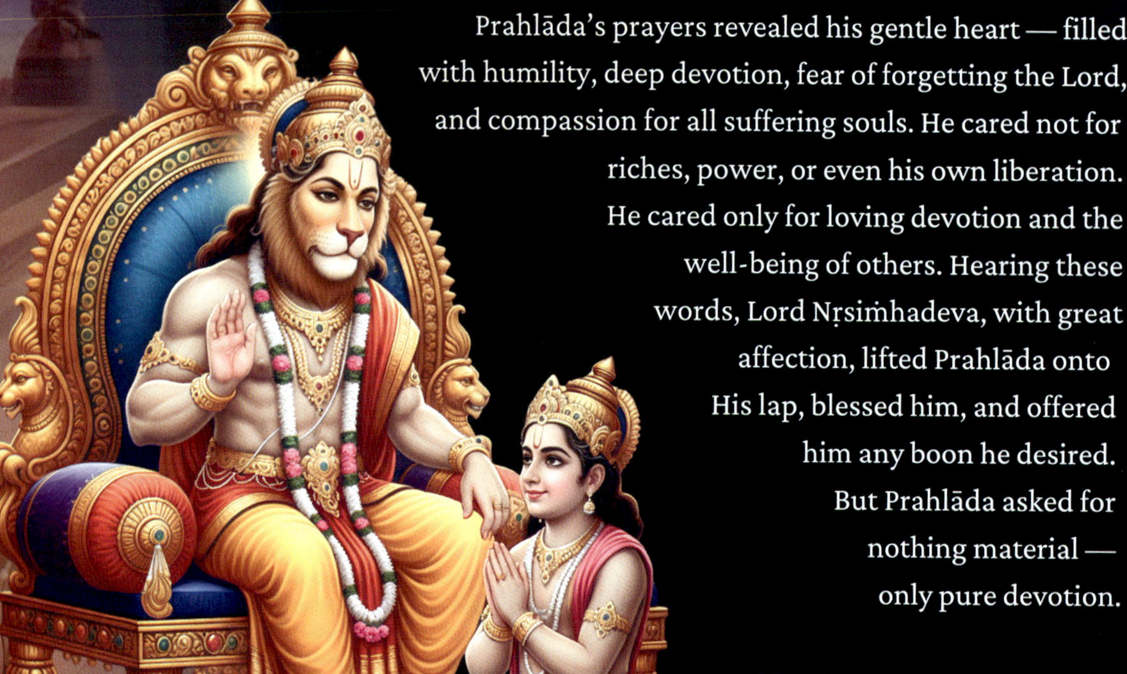

Prahlāda's prayers revealed his gentle heart — filled with humility, deep devotion, fear of forgetting the Lord, and compassion for all suffering souls. He cared not for riches, power, or even his own liberation. He cared only for loving devotion and the well-being of others. Hearing these words, Lord Nṛsiṁhadeva, with great affection, lifted Prahlāda onto His lap, blessed him, and offered him any boon he desired. But Prahlāda asked for nothing material — only pure devotion.

*Selfless devotees are satisfied with their devotion, but pray for the wellbeing of others.*

# 6. Śrīla Prabhupāda's Prayers of Dependence

In 1965, at the age of 69, Śrīla A.C. Bhaktivedanta Swami Prabhupāda left India to carry Lord Caitanya's message to the Western world. He had no money, no followers, and no comfort — only a small trunk of books, some clothes, and deep faith in Lord Kṛṣṇa.

He boarded a cargo ship called the Jaladuta in Calcutta. The journey across the ocean was very rough. Twice, Prabhupāda suffered severe heart attacks on the ship. He was weak and in great pain, but instead of feeling discouraged, he folded his hands and prayed to Lord Kṛṣṇa with all sincerity.

In his diary, he wrote beautiful prayers in Bengali: "O Lord Kṛṣṇa, I am like a puppet in Your hands. Please make me dance, make me dance, as You wish. I have no power on my own, but if You give me strength, then people all over the world will hear about You and chant Your holy names."

He prayed not for his health, wealth, or safety, but only for the chance to glorify Kṛṣṇa. This mood of pure prayer is the essence of Vandanam. Kṛṣṇa heard his prayers, and not only saved him from seasickness and heart attacks on Jaladuta, but also empowered him to spread bhakti all over the world. After reaching America, though he began alone and unknown, Prabhupāda's prayers and devotion attracted many young people. Within just a few years, the sound of Hare Kṛṣṇa spread to every continent.

*Real prayer is asking to serve Kṛṣṇa in any situation.*

# LET'S PRAY!

*Vandanam*, or offering heartfelt prayers, is a very special way to connect with Kṛṣṇa. Just as Gajendra prayed in danger, Akrūra prayed in anticipation, Kuntī prayed in gratitude, Dhruva prayed in transformation, and Prahlāda prayed in compassion — we too can pray in our own simple words.

Prayer is like opening the door of our heart to Kṛṣṇa and saying, "Please come in." It is not about fancy words or long verses, but about sincerity and humility.

## BENEFITS OF VANDANAM

| | | |
|---|---|---|
| 1 | CONNECTION | Prayer keeps our relationship with Kṛṣṇa alive and strong. |
| 2 | HUMILITY | It softens pride and helps us see ourselves as dependent on Him. |
| 3 | PEACE | By unburdening our worries at His feet, our hearts feel lighter. |
| 4 | STRENGTH | Prayer gives us courage in times of fear & direction in times of confusion. |
| 5 | COMPASSION | Prayers can turn self-centeredness into care for others. |
| 6 | GRATITUDE | Remembering Kṛṣṇa's kindness makes us thankful and joyful. |

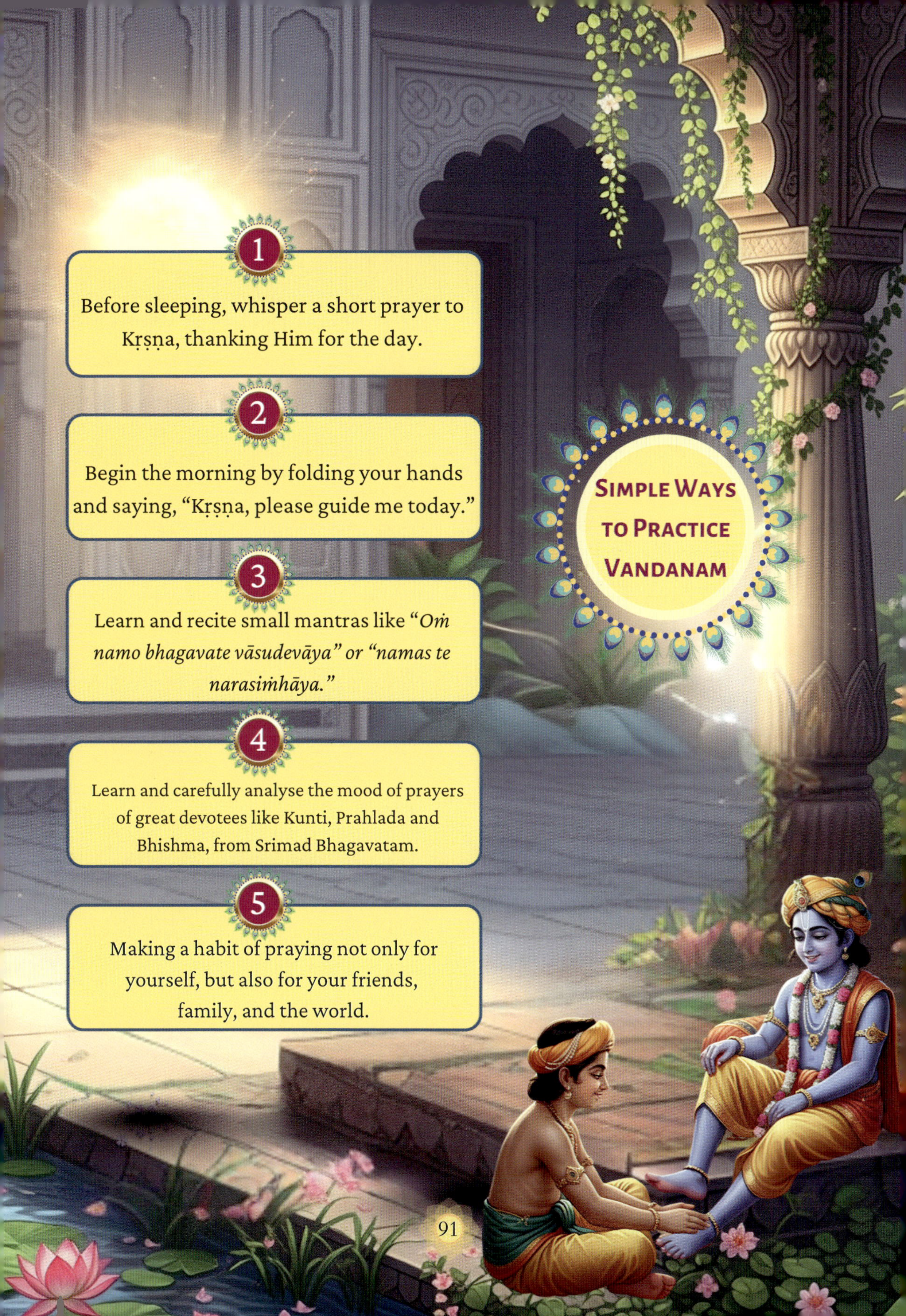



**1**

Before sleeping, whisper a short prayer to Kṛṣṇa, thanking Him for the day.

**2**

Begin the morning by folding your hands and saying, "Kṛṣṇa, please guide me today."

**3**

Learn and recite small mantras like "*Oṁ namo bhagavate vāsudevāya*" or "*namas te narasiṁhāya.*"

**4**

Learn and carefully analyse the mood of prayers of great devotees like Kunti, Prahlada and Bhishma, from Srimad Bhagavatam.

**5**

Making a habit of praying not only for yourself, but also for your friends, family, and the world.

# 7

# DĀSYAṀ

## SERVICE

*Selfless and grateful service to Kṛṣṇa
is the soul's real happiness.*

*Dāsyaṁ* means service. Our true spiritual identity is to serve the Supreme Lord Kṛṣṇa in the mood of humble servants. The scriptures declare: *"jīvera svarūpa haya — kṛṣṇera nitya dāsa:* The soul's real nature is to be the eternal servant of Kṛṣṇa." (CC Madhya 20.108)

Lord Caitanya teaches us that every soul is meant to be a servant of Lord Kṛṣṇa. He says this in a beautiful prayer:

> *ayi nanda-tanuja kiṅkaraṁ  patitaṁ māṁ viṣame bhavāmbudhau*
> *kṛpayā tava pāda-paṅkaja- sthita-dhūlī-sadṛśaṁ vicintaya*

"O Kṛṣṇa, dear son of Nanda Mahārāja, I am Your servant forever. But because of my own mistakes, I have fallen into the big, dangerous ocean of this material world. Please be merciful and think of me as just a tiny speck of dust at Your lotus feet." (Śikṣāṣṭakam 5)

In this world, the word "servant" often sounds lowly or demeaning. But in spiritual life, being a servant is the most exalted position! Service to the Lord or His devotees is never forced or born of fear. It is an expression of love, and a way to deepen that love. Just as we naturally serve those we care about—a mother serves her child, a friend serves his companion, a beloved serves the one dearest to them—devotees joyfully serve Kṛṣṇa out of affection.

> *kṛṣṇa-dāsa-abhimāne ye ānanda-sindhu*
> *koṭī-brahma-sukha nahe tāra eka bindu*

"The happiness of being Kṛṣṇa's servant is like an ocean of joy. Even if the bliss of impersonal Brahman liberation were multiplied ten million times, it could not equal a single drop of this joy." (CC Ādi 6.44)

There are many kinds of devotees: some serve Kṛṣṇa as servants (*dāsya-bhaktas*), some as friends (*sakhya-bhaktas*), some as parents (*vātsalya-bhaktas*), and some as beloveds (*mādhurya-bhaktas*). Their moods differ, but all have one thing in common—service. Without service, *bhakti* is incomplete.

If there is any position higher than being Kṛṣṇa's servant, it is being the servant of His servant. Still more exalted is being the servant of the servant of the servant. In the spiritual world, the hierarchy is opposite to this world. Here, everyone wants to be the master. There, the closer one comes to being a servant of the servants of Kṛṣṇa, the greater the joy and fortune.

In the material world, a master enjoys more comforts than a servant. But in the spiritual world, the servants of Kṛṣṇa experience greater joy than even the Lord Himself. The best example is Śrīmatī Rādhārāṇī, the topmost servant of Kṛṣṇa. Seeing how She enjoys even more happiness in serving Him than He does in receiving service, Kṛṣṇa became curious. To taste this mystery and experience Her joy, Kṛṣṇa appeared as Śrī Caitanya Mahāprabhu, entering into Her mood of love.

In the *Bhāgavatam*, Prahlāda Mahārāja prays to Lord Nṛsiṁhadeva: "The problems of this world seem endless, and the solutions often create more trouble than the problems themselves. The only true solution is to engage in Your service."

Cultivating this mood of service makes our hearts joyful, and the challenges of this world no longer disturb us. After many lifetimes, the most fortunate souls come to this simple realization: "I am Kṛṣṇa's eternal servant." Here are some glorious examples of devotees who served the Lord with dedication and devotion.

### THREE LEVELS OF SERVANTS

| BEST SERVANT | MEDIOCRE SERVANT | WORST SERVANT |
| --- | --- | --- |
| Accomplishes more than the duty entrusted by the master. | Does only what the master orders, never going beyond, though capable. | Fails to carry out the master's order, even though able. |

# 1. Hanumān – The Servant who served with all his strength

Hanumān is celebrated as the very symbol of service in the pastimes of Lord Rāma. When Mother Sītā-devī was kidnapped by the demon Rāvaṇa and taken to Laṅkā, Lord Rāma entrusted Hanumān with the sacred mission of finding Her.

With unshakable determination, Hanumān leapt across the mighty ocean — a task impossible for anyone. He succeeded not by his strength, but by remembering Rāma and considering himself nothing more than an arrow released from Rāma's bow.

In Laṅkā, Hanumān discovered Sītā-devī in the Aśoka grove. He consoled Her with sweet words of hope, assuring Her that Lord Rāma would soon come to rescue Her. But Hanumān did not stop there. As a first-class servant, he went further. To warn the demons, he destroyed the Aśoka garden. When captured and brought before Rāvaṇa, Hanumān fearlessly declared: "I am the servant of Lord Rāma!"

Even when his tail was set on fire, Hanumān turned that situation into service. He leapt from roof to roof, using his blazing tail to set the city of Laṅkā ablaze, striking terror in the hearts of the demons and showing the power of one servant of Rāma.

Later, during the great war, when Rāma and Lakṣmaṇa fell unconscious in battle, Hanumān carried the entire mountain of healing herbs to save their lives and protect the army. Finally, when Rāma was crowned king in Ayodhyā, Hanumān stood humbly by His side — not proud of his mighty deeds, but simply grateful.

*The greatest strength does not come from muscle or might, but from serving the Lord with love, humility, and devotion.*

# 2. Śrī Balarāma – The One who serves in every way

Śrī Balarāma is Lord Kṛṣṇa's elder brother and, at the same time, the Servitor Godhead. In the spiritual world, He is Kṛṣṇa's first expansion. From Him come the *catur-vyūha* expansions and the puruṣa-avatāras. Yet, despite His greatness, Balarāma finds His highest joy in serving Kṛṣṇa.

Balarāma's service is unique because He serves the Lord in every *rasa*—every loving relationship with Kṛṣṇa:

### In Śānta-rasa (neutrality):

Balarāma expands Himself to create the very setting for Kṛṣṇa's pastimes. The land of Goloka Vṛndāvana, its forests, rivers, gardens, mountains, and the blissful atmosphere —all are manifestations of Balarāma's service, arranged for Kṛṣṇa's pleasure.

### In Dāsya-rasa (servitude):

Balarāma carries out whatever is required for Kṛṣṇa. He builds, protects, supports, and provides. The ground Kṛṣṇa walks upon, the seats He rests on, the sandals and ornaments He wears—all are Balarāma's arrangements. As Śeṣa Nāga, He even becomes Kṛṣṇa's divine bed and canopy.

### In Sakhya-rasa (friendship):

Balarāma is Kṛṣṇa's dearest playmate. They herd the cows side by side, wrestle, joke, and eat lunch together in the forest. Their laughter and friendship know no limits.

### In Vātsalya-rasa (parental affection):

As the elder brother, Balarāma lovingly guides and protects Kṛṣṇa. He often takes responsibility like a parent—watching over Him during Their forest adventures.

### In Mādhurya-rasa (conjugal love):

Balarāma expands as Ananga Mañjari, the younger sister of Śrīmatī Rādhārāṇī, to assist in the most intimate pastimes of Rādhā and Kṛṣṇa.

Thus, Balarāma's service spirit is all-encompassing. True perfection of service means to use everything we have—body, mind, words, and possessions—in the Lord's service.

*The greatest joy lies in serving Kṛṣṇa in every possible way.*

# 3. Lakṣmaṇa – The Brother Who Served Without Rest

When Lord Rāma, the prince of Ayodhyā, was ordered to spend fourteen years in the forest, everyone in the palace was shocked and heartbroken. Yet without a moment's hesitation, Lakṣmaṇa, Rāma's younger brother, vowed to accompany Him. Though he was under no obligation to go, Lakṣmaṇa could not imagine life apart from his Lord.

Though born a prince, Lakṣmaṇa happily gave up his palace, soft bed, and royal comforts to live in the rough forests. To him, serving Rāma was the greatest treasure.

During those long years of exile, Lakṣmaṇa tirelessly served Rāma and Sītā-devī. He built huts, fetched water, gathered fruits, and stood guard with his bow always ready. He remained awake night after night, protecting them from wild animals and lurking demons. It is said that for the entire fourteen years, Lakṣmaṇa did not close his eyes to sleep — his love kept him alert, always watching over his beloved Lord.

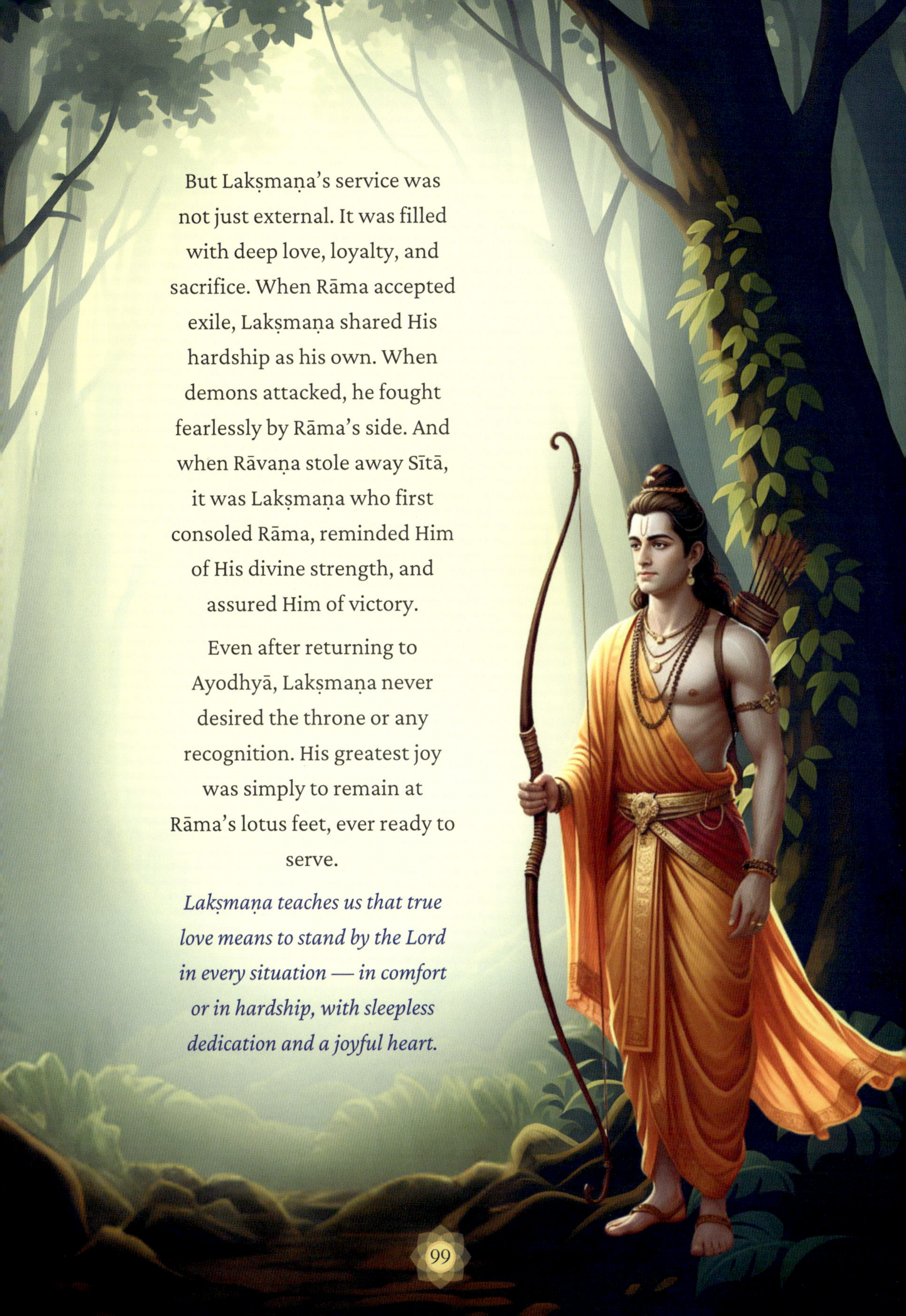

But Lakṣmaṇa's service was not just external. It was filled with deep love, loyalty, and sacrifice. When Rāma accepted exile, Lakṣmaṇa shared His hardship as his own. When demons attacked, he fought fearlessly by Rāma's side. And when Rāvaṇa stole away Sītā, it was Lakṣmaṇa who first consoled Rāma, reminded Him of His divine strength, and assured Him of victory.

Even after returning to Ayodhyā, Lakṣmaṇa never desired the throne or any recognition. His greatest joy was simply to remain at Rāma's lotus feet, ever ready to serve.

*Lakṣmaṇa teaches us that true love means to stand by the Lord in every situation — in comfort or in hardship, with sleepless dedication and a joyful heart.*

# 4. Girirāja Govardhana
## The Hill that Serves with Humility

In Vṛndāvana there is a most sacred hill called Govardhana. But Govardhana is not just a hill — he is a great devotee who constantly serves Lord Kṛṣṇa.

Every day, Govardhana offers his service in many wonderful ways. He provides soft, sweet grasses for Kṛṣṇa's cows, crystal-clear water in lakes and ponds, shady caves for rest, and beautiful flowers and fruits for enjoyment. His very body is filled with jewels, minerals, and dust softer than silk, which give great pleasure to the Lord's lotus feet.

When Kṛṣṇa played in Vṛndāvana with the gopas, Govardhana gave them grassy seats, cool caves to relax in, and refreshing streams to quench their thirst. He felt immense joy in providing everything the Lord and His devotees needed. In this way, Govardhana showed that service is complete not only when we serve Kṛṣṇa directly but also when we serve His devotees. Because of this, Śrīmatī Rādhārāṇī lovingly gave Govardhana the title *"Haridāsa-varya"* — the best among the servants of the Lord.

Govardhana's greatest service came during the famous pastime of lifting Govardhana Hill. When Indra, the king of heaven, became angry because the *Vrajavāsīs* stopped his worship, he sent furious storms — dark clouds, heavy rains, and roaring thunder — to destroy Vṛndāvana. Terrified, the Vrajavasis ran to Kṛṣṇa for shelter.

Smiling, Kṛṣṇa effortlessly lifted Govardhana Hill with the little finger of His left hand, just as a child might lift a toy umbrella. All the residents of Vṛndāvana, along with their cows and calves, took refuge beneath the hill. For seven days and nights, Govardhana stood strong on Kṛṣṇa's finger, becoming a giant umbrella of love and protection. Indra too was a servant of Kṛṣṇa, but in his pride he forgot his true position.

Govardhana, on the other hand, served with humility. To show that humble service is greater than proud power, Kṛṣṇa stopped Indra's worship and inaugurated the festival of Govardhana Pūjā, establishing Girirāja as the true servant of the Lord.

Even today, pilgrims walk around Govardhana Hill (*Govardhana-parikramā*), remembering his glorious service and praying for his blessings — that they too may serve Kṛṣṇa with the same humility and selflessness.

*The best servant is the one who not only serves the Lord but also protects and cares for His devotees.*

# Let's Serve!

*Dāsyaṁ* reminds us that the greatest honor in life is not to be a master, but to be a servant of the Supreme Lord. Whether it is Hanumān leaping across the ocean for Rāma, Lakṣmaṇa staying awake for 14 years to serve his brother, Arjuna letting Kṛṣṇa guide his chariot, Uddhava carrying Kṛṣṇa's message, or Girirāja Govardhana providing shade, water, fruits, and shelter for the *Vrajavāsīs* — all of them found their joy and strength in service.

Even the Supreme Lord Himself admires this mood. Śrīmatī Rādhārāṇī feels greater happiness in serving Kṛṣṇa than He feels in being served, and Kṛṣṇa became Śrī Caitanya Mahāprabhu just to taste the sweetness of Her service.

This shows us how exalted and blissful the mood of dāsya truly is. Service is not a burden. It is the most natural and joyful way to express our love for Kṛṣṇa.

## Benefits of Dāsyaṁ

| # | | |
|---|---|---|
| 1 | **Peace** | Problems of the world no longer disturb the servant of Kṛṣṇa. |
| 2 | **Joy** | Serving the Lord brings deeper joy than worldly comfort. |
| 3 | **Strength** | The servant feels fearless, knowing the Lord is the protector. |
| 4 | **Humility** | Service removes pride and makes the heart soft. |
| 5 | **Connection** | Service deepens our relationship with Kṛṣṇa and His devotees. |
| 6 | **Purification** | By serving, the heart becomes clean of selfish desires. |

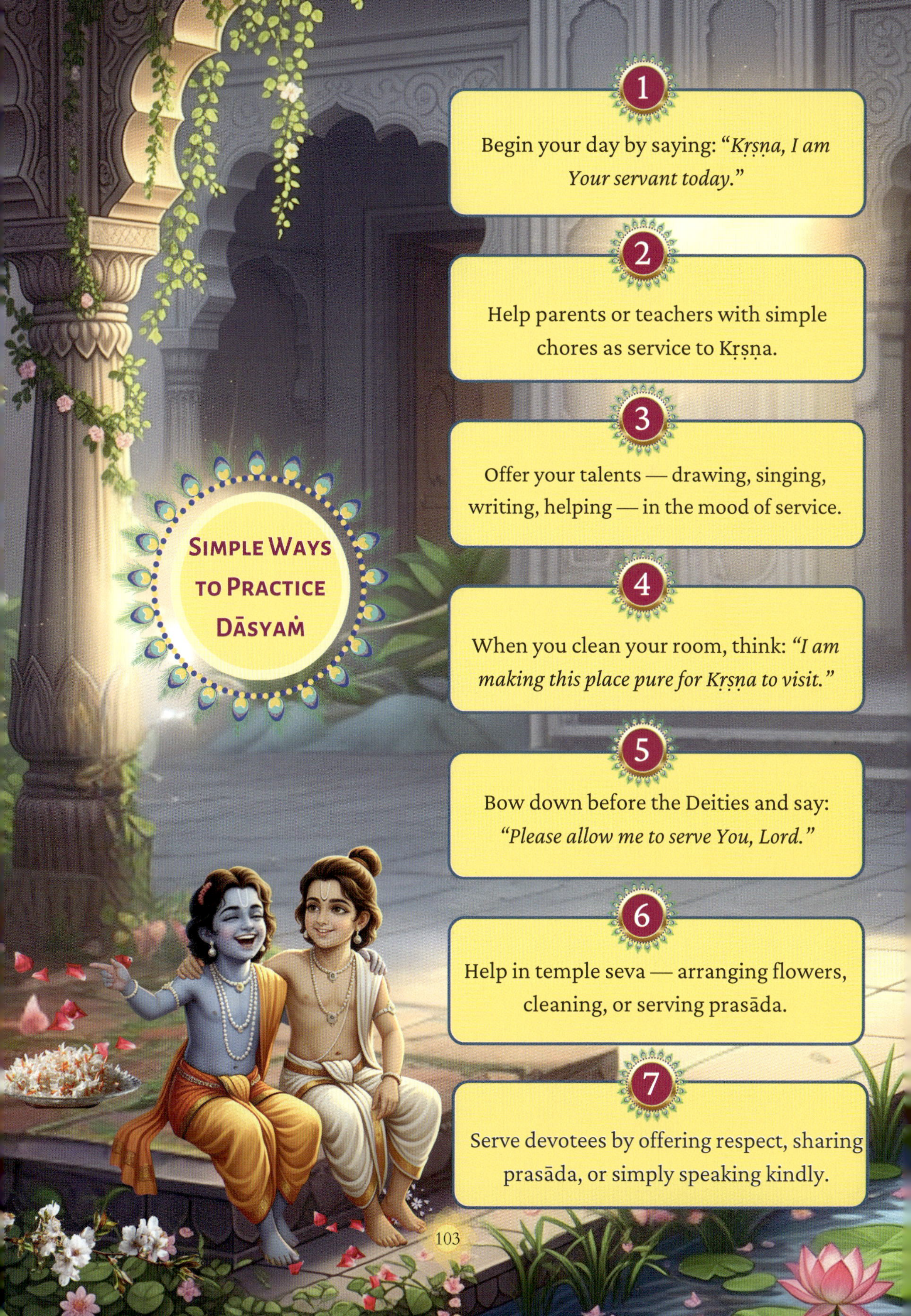


Simple Ways to Practice Dāsyaṁ

1
Begin your day by saying: "Kṛṣṇa, I am Your servant today."

2
Help parents or teachers with simple chores as service to Kṛṣṇa.

3
Offer your talents — drawing, singing, writing, helping — in the mood of service.

4
When you clean your room, think: "I am making this place pure for Kṛṣṇa to visit."

5
Bow down before the Deities and say: "Please allow me to serve You, Lord."

6
Help in temple seva — arranging flowers, cleaning, or serving prasāda.

7
Serve devotees by offering respect, sharing prasāda, or simply speaking kindly.

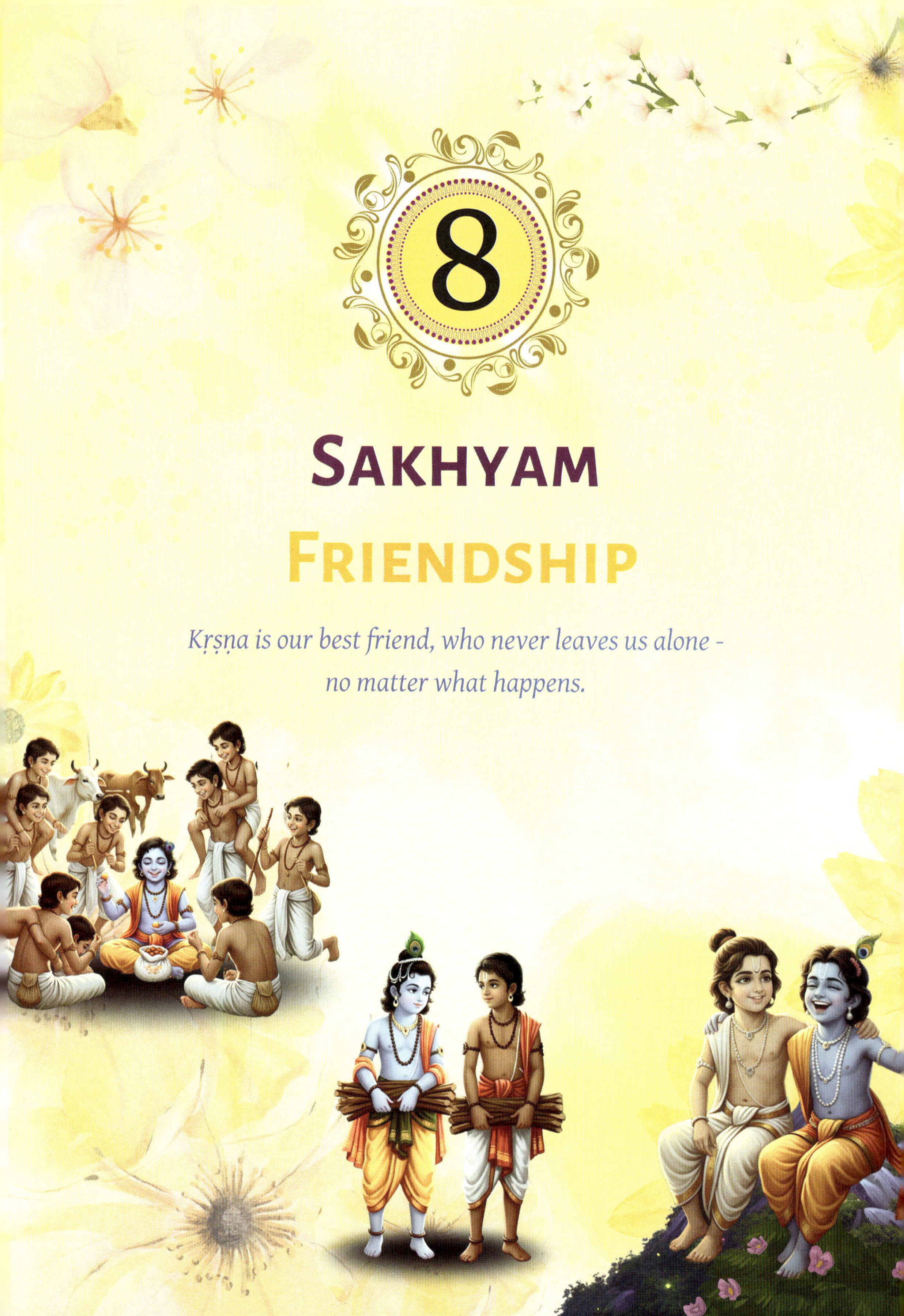

# 8

# Sakhyam

# Friendship

*Kṛṣṇa is our best friend, who never leaves us alone -
no matter what happens.*

Imagine this — the all-powerful creator of the universe, the protector of everyone, the most beautiful and loving Lord, wants to be your best friend! At first it might sound surprising, because we are tiny souls and He is the Almighty. And in the previous chapter we learned that we are His eternal servants. So how can we also be His friends? That is the beauty of spiritual life: in bhakti, service can blossom into friendship, and friendship itself becomes a way of serving with love.

Kṛṣṇa Himself declares in the *Bhagavad-gītā (5.29)*: *suhṛdaṁ sarva-bhūtānāṁ* — "I am the dearest friend and well-wisher of all living beings."

The scriptures compare the soul and the Lord to two birds sitting in the same tree. One bird (the soul) eats the fruits—sometimes sweet, sometimes bitter—while the other bird (the Lord) simply watches, always ready to guide and protect. In truth, Kṛṣṇa has always been our best friend. We only need to recognize Him as such.

Friendship (*sakhyam*) is more intimate than servitude (*dāsyam*). A servant reveres his master from a distance, but a friend sits beside his friend, laughs with him, plays with him, and freely shares joys and sorrows. In sakhya, there is less formality and awe, and more closeness, affection, and trust.

So how can a practicing devotee cultivate friendship with Kṛṣṇa? Not by pretending to be His equal, but by opening our hearts to Him. Just as you share your secrets, dreams, and worries with your closest friend, you can talk to Kṛṣṇa the same way—telling Him your joys and sorrows, asking for His help, and walking through life with Him by your side.

In fact, for a devotee, the Lord is everything, as expressed in this famous prayer:

*tvam eva mātā ca pitā tvam eva*

*tvam eva bandhuś ca sakhā tvam eva*

*tvam eva vidyā draviṇaṁ tvam eva*

*tvam eva sarvaṁ mama deva-deva*

"O Lord of Lords, You are my mother. You are my father. You are my relative. You are my friend. You are my wisdom. You are my wealth, You are my everything."

And just like friends exchange gifts, we too can offer something to Kṛṣṇa — a leaf, a flower, a fruit, or even a little water — with simple, friendly affection. In return, He offers us His eternal friendship, love, and protection.

## 1. Gopas Who Treat Kṛṣṇa as Their Equal

In Vṛndāvana, Kṛṣṇa's days were full of fun with His dearest friends — the cowherd boys like Śrīdāmā, Sudāmā, Subala, Stoka Kṛṣṇa, Madhumaṅgala, and many others. They were of the same age as Him, and they never thought of Him as the Supreme Lord. For them, He was simply their best friend!

Every morning, the boys would gather with their sticks, flutes, and little lunches tied up in cloth pouches. With joyful shouts, they accompany Kṛṣṇa to the forest along with their cows. Together they ran, laughed, and filled the meadows of Vṛndāvana with music and cheer. They praise Kṛṣṇa's adventures of killing demons.

Their friendship was so natural that they treated Kṛṣṇa as one of them. Sometimes they wrestled in play — and whoever lost had to carry the winner on his shoulders.

Even the Supreme Lord Kṛṣṇa happily carried His friends on His shoulders when He lost a match! At lunchtime, they all sat in a circle, opening their packets of rice, fruits, and sweets. They would share with each other — "Here, taste mine, it's delicious!" And Kṛṣṇa too would give them His food, laughing and enjoying like an ordinary boy.

The cowherd boys didn't fold hands to pray or stand at a distance in awe. They climbed on His shoulders, joked with Him, and even teased Him and scolded Him at times. EVen if Kṛṣṇa manifests His powers and protect them from dangerous demons, venomous snakes and forest fires, they consider Kṛṣṇa as their equal, and not God! That is the nature of their friendship.

*The cowherd boys share an intimate bonding with Kṛṣṇa without reverence.*

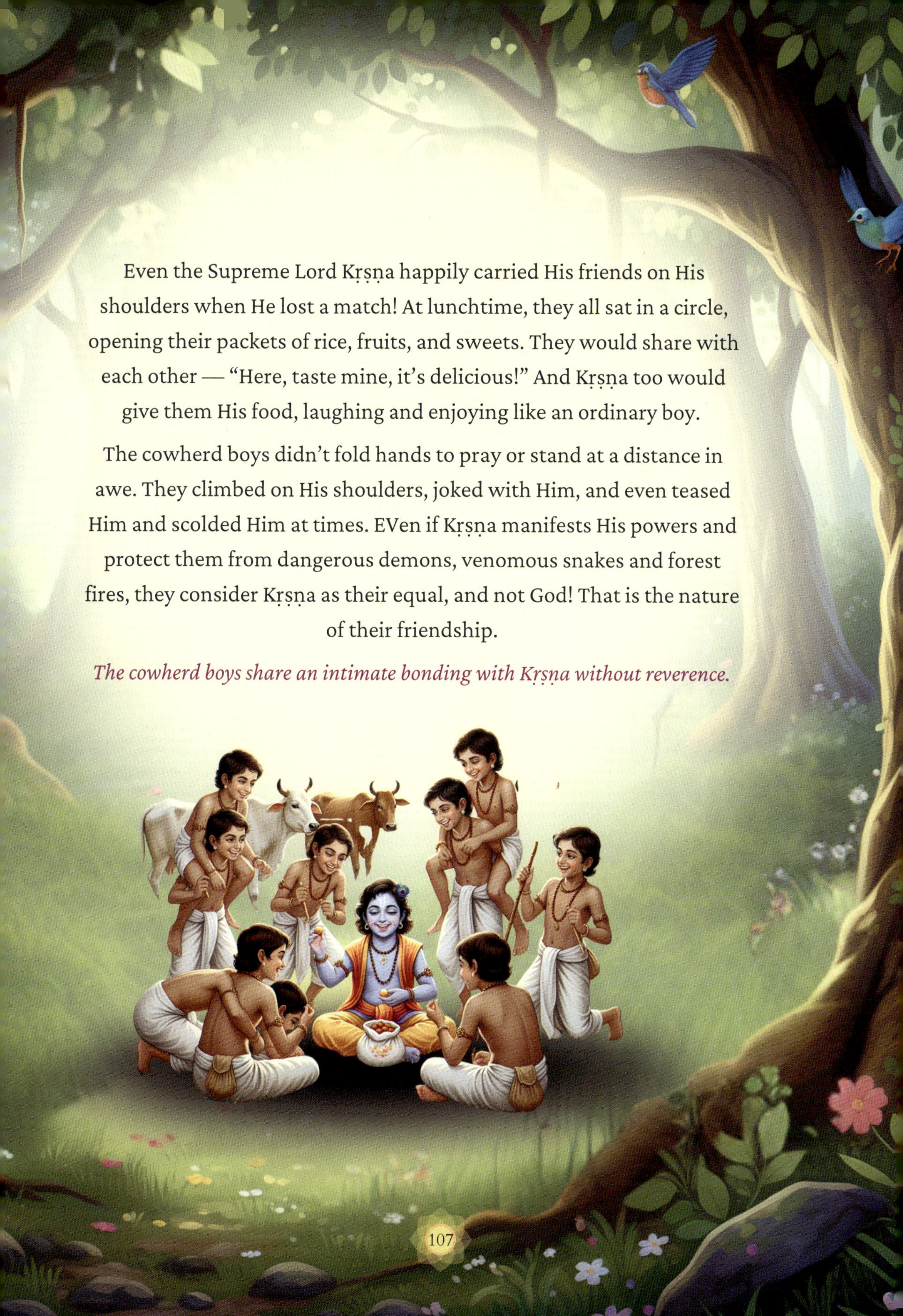

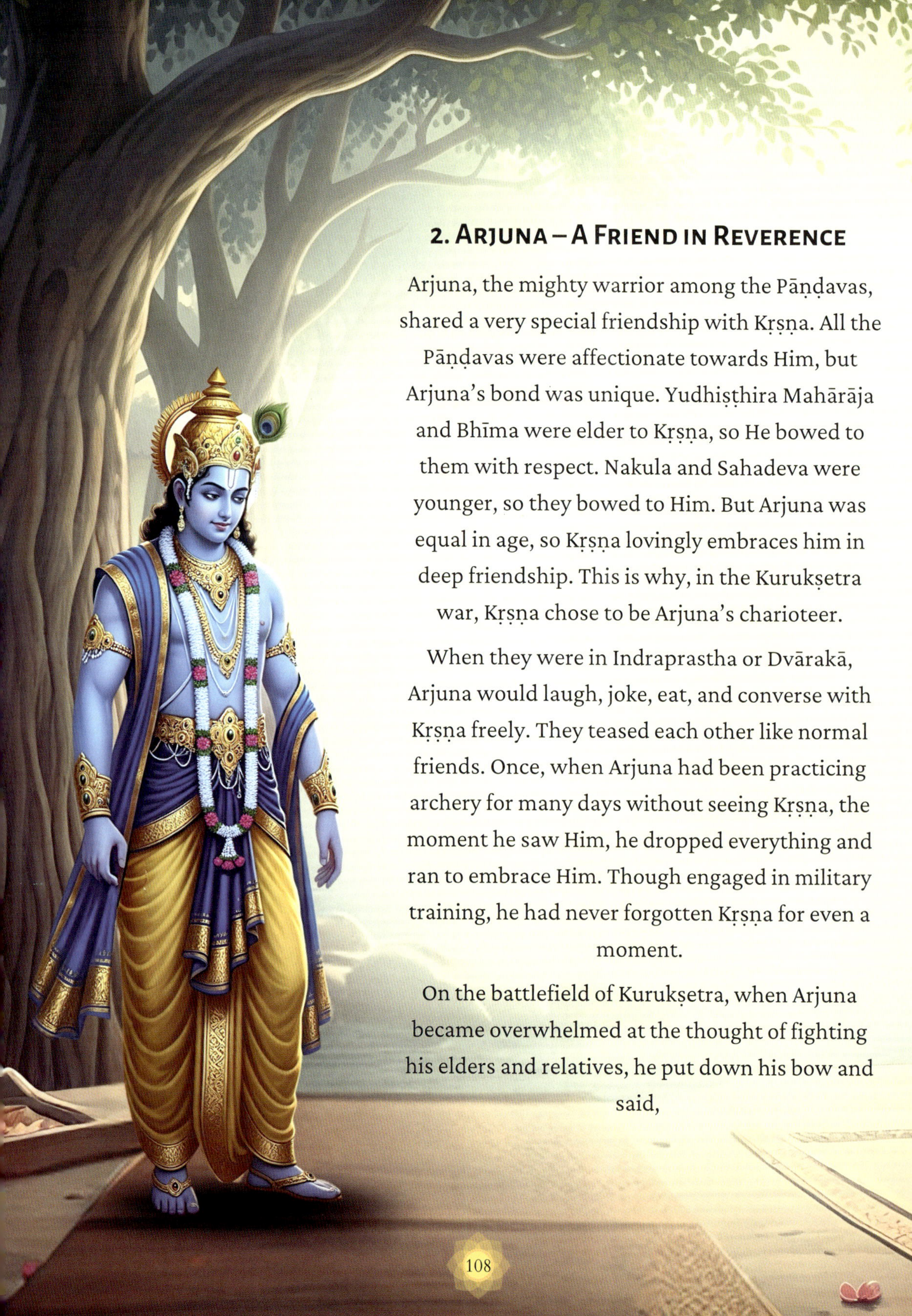

## 2. Arjuna – A Friend in Reverence

Arjuna, the mighty warrior among the Pāṇḍavas, shared a very special friendship with Kṛṣṇa. All the Pāṇḍavas were affectionate towards Him, but Arjuna's bond was unique. Yudhiṣṭhira Mahārāja and Bhīma were elder to Kṛṣṇa, so He bowed to them with respect. Nakula and Sahadeva were younger, so they bowed to Him. But Arjuna was equal in age, so Kṛṣṇa lovingly embraces him in deep friendship. This is why, in the Kurukṣetra war, Kṛṣṇa chose to be Arjuna's charioteer.

When they were in Indraprastha or Dvārakā, Arjuna would laugh, joke, eat, and converse with Kṛṣṇa freely. They teased each other like normal friends. Once, when Arjuna had been practicing archery for many days without seeing Kṛṣṇa, the moment he saw Him, he dropped everything and ran to embrace Him. Though engaged in military training, he had never forgotten Kṛṣṇa for even a moment.

On the battlefield of Kurukṣetra, when Arjuna became overwhelmed at the thought of fighting his elders and relatives, he put down his bow and said,

"Kṛṣṇa, I cannot fight." Kṛṣṇa then revealed the supreme wisdom of the Bhagavad-gītā, telling him, "You are My devotee and My dear friend; therefore I am revealing this supreme secret to you." (BG 4.3)

At one point in the war, Aśvatthāmā wickedly attacked Kṛṣṇa, even though He was acting only as a charioteer. Seeing this, Arjuna leapt forward to shield Kṛṣṇa with his own body, ready to take all the arrows upon himself. To him, the piercing arrows felt like showers of flowers, because he was filled with ecstatic love for his dearest friend.

After Kṛṣṇa departed from this world, Arjuna remembered their intimate moments with tears: "We joked, ate together, rested

together, and sometimes I treated Him as an equal." Yet he also knew that Kṛṣṇa was the Supreme Lord, and he begged forgiveness for the times he had spoken too casually.

This highlights the special nature of Arjuna's friendship. Unlike the cowherd boys of Vṛndāvana, who knew only intimacy and no reverence, Arjuna's sakhya mixed closeness with awe and respect. He treated Kṛṣṇa as his equal and beloved companion, yet also recognized Him as the Supreme Personality of Godhead.

Friendship with Kṛṣṇa means walking with Him through life — with love, trust, and reverence.

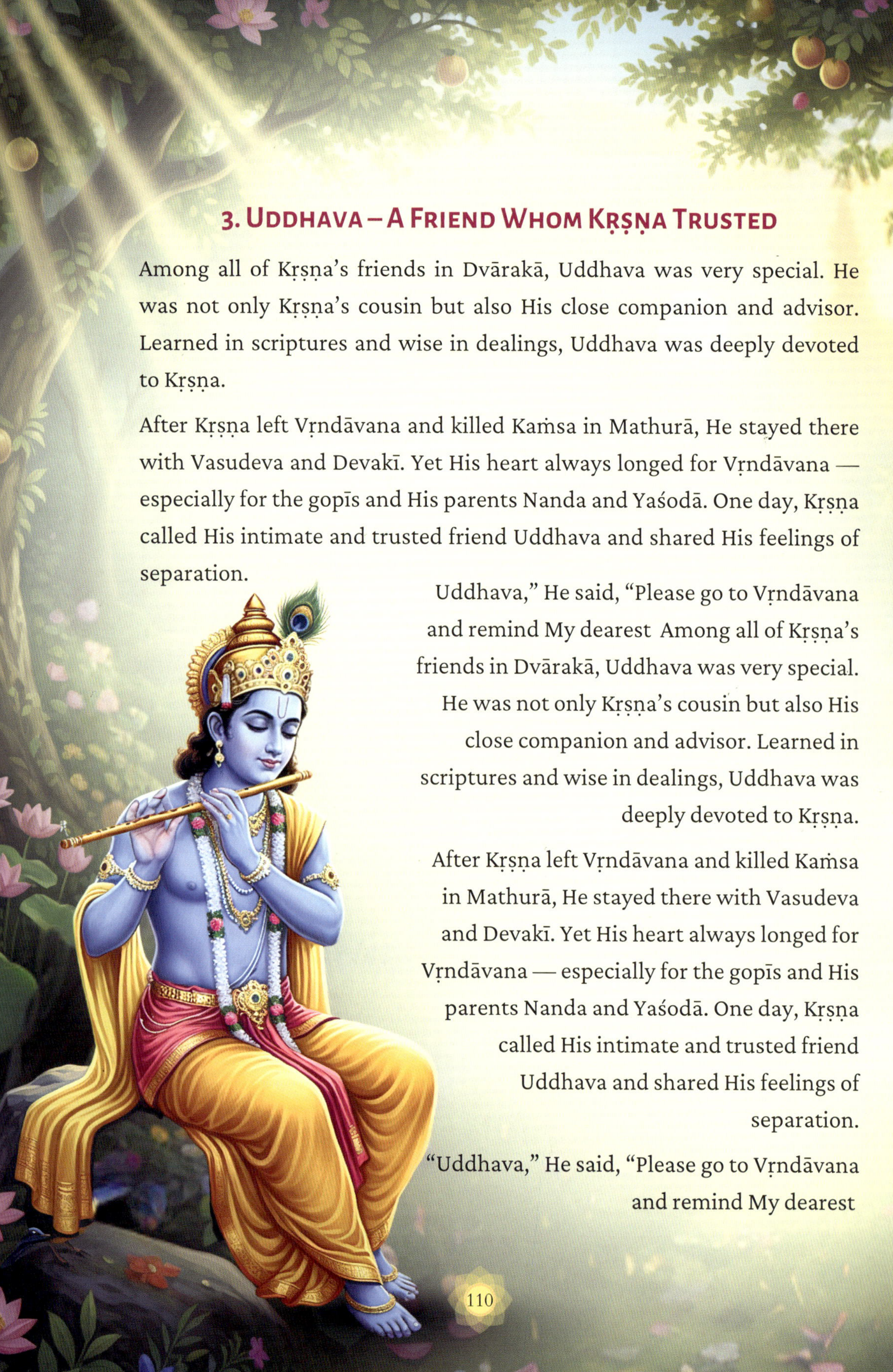

### 3. UDDHAVA – A FRIEND WHOM KṚṢṆA TRUSTED

Among all of Kṛṣṇa's friends in Dvārakā, Uddhava was very special. He was not only Kṛṣṇa's cousin but also His close companion and advisor. Learned in scriptures and wise in dealings, Uddhava was deeply devoted to Kṛṣṇa.

After Kṛṣṇa left Vṛndāvana and killed Kaṁsa in Mathurā, He stayed there with Vasudeva and Devakī. Yet His heart always longed for Vṛndāvana — especially for the gopīs and His parents Nanda and Yaśodā. One day, Kṛṣṇa called His intimate and trusted friend Uddhava and shared His feelings of separation.

Uddhava," He said, "Please go to Vṛndāvana and remind My dearest Among all of Kṛṣṇa's friends in Dvārakā, Uddhava was very special. He was not only Kṛṣṇa's cousin but also His close companion and advisor. Learned in scriptures and wise in dealings, Uddhava was deeply devoted to Kṛṣṇa.

After Kṛṣṇa left Vṛndāvana and killed Kaṁsa in Mathurā, He stayed there with Vasudeva and Devakī. Yet His heart always longed for Vṛndāvana — especially for the gopīs and His parents Nanda and Yaśodā. One day, Kṛṣṇa called His intimate and trusted friend Uddhava and shared His feelings of separation.

"Uddhava," He said, "Please go to Vṛndāvana and remind My dearest devotees that I am always with them, and they are always in My thoughts. I miss them so much and can never forget them. Console them and give them strength with My words."

Such a confidential message to His topmost devotees shows how trusted Uddhava was to Kṛṣṇa.

When Uddhava arrived in Vṛndāvana, he was astonished. He saw how the gopīs' love for Kṛṣṇa was so deep that they thought of nothing else — every tree, every breeze reminded them of Him. He listened to their songs of longing, and his heart melted.

Uddhava realized, "I came here to console them, but I am the one being inspired by their intense, selfless devotion! Their love for Kṛṣṇa is far beyond anything I have ever known."

Uddhava returned to Kṛṣṇa with a humbled heart, carrying not only the Lord's message but also the priceless lesson of pure, selfless friendship and devotion.

*Trusted friends of Kṛṣṇa carry His messages effectively, and inspire His devotees.*

# 4. Sudāmā – Poor in Wealth, but Rich in Love

Sudāmā was a poor *brāhmaṇa* — simple, gentle, and deeply devoted. But above all, he was Kṛṣṇa's lifelong friend. As children, they had studied together in the gurukula of Sandīpani Muni, playing and learning side by side.

Years later, Sudāmā lived in poverty with his wife. One day she said, "Please go to Dvārakā and see your dear friend Kṛṣṇa. Surely He will help us." Sudāmā hesitated — how could he approach the King of Dvārakā empty-handed? At last, he carried a tiny bundle of flat rice, begged from his neighbors.

When Sudāmā arrived, Kṛṣṇa saw him from afar and ran to greet him with tears of joy. The Supreme Lord embraced His old friend tightly, washed his feet with His own hands, and seated him with honor, while Queen Rukmiṇī herself fanned him with a *chamara*.

Sudāmā felt shy and hid his small bundle of rice, thinking it unworthy as a gift. But Kṛṣṇa, knowing his heart, snatched it joyfully. "Ah, my dear friend has brought Me something so precious!" He exclaimed, and ate a handful with delight. Just by tasting that simple offering, the Lord blessed Sudāmā's family with immense wealth and comfort.

When Sudāmā returned home, his hut had been transformed into a palace. Yet he felt no pride. His greatest treasure was not the riches, but the loving friendship of Lord Kṛṣṇa.

*Kṛṣṇa doesn't look at the size of our gift, but at the love with which we offer it.*

# Let's Befriend!

Kṛṣṇa is not only the Supreme Lord but also our closest and dearest friend. Whether it was the cowherd boys of Vṛndāvana playing with Him, Sudāmā offering a handful of flat rice, or Arjuna receiving guidance on the battlefield, their lives show that friendship with Kṛṣṇa fills the hearts with satisfaction and devotion.

Friendship with Kṛṣṇa means opening our heart to Him — sharing our joys, fears, secrets, and dreams, just as we do with our best friends. And the most beautiful part is: Kṛṣṇa never forgets His friends, and He never leaves their side.

## Benefits of Sakhyam

| | | |
|---|---|---|
| 1 | Trust | We gain unshakable confidence on Kṛṣṇa's protection. |
| 2 | Joy | Life becomes light when we see Kṛṣṇa as well wisher. |
| 3 | Guidance | We receive wisdom and clarity in confusing times. |
| 4 | Strength | We feel courage to face any challenge. |
| 5 | Intimacy | Our relationship with the Lord grows deeper & personal |

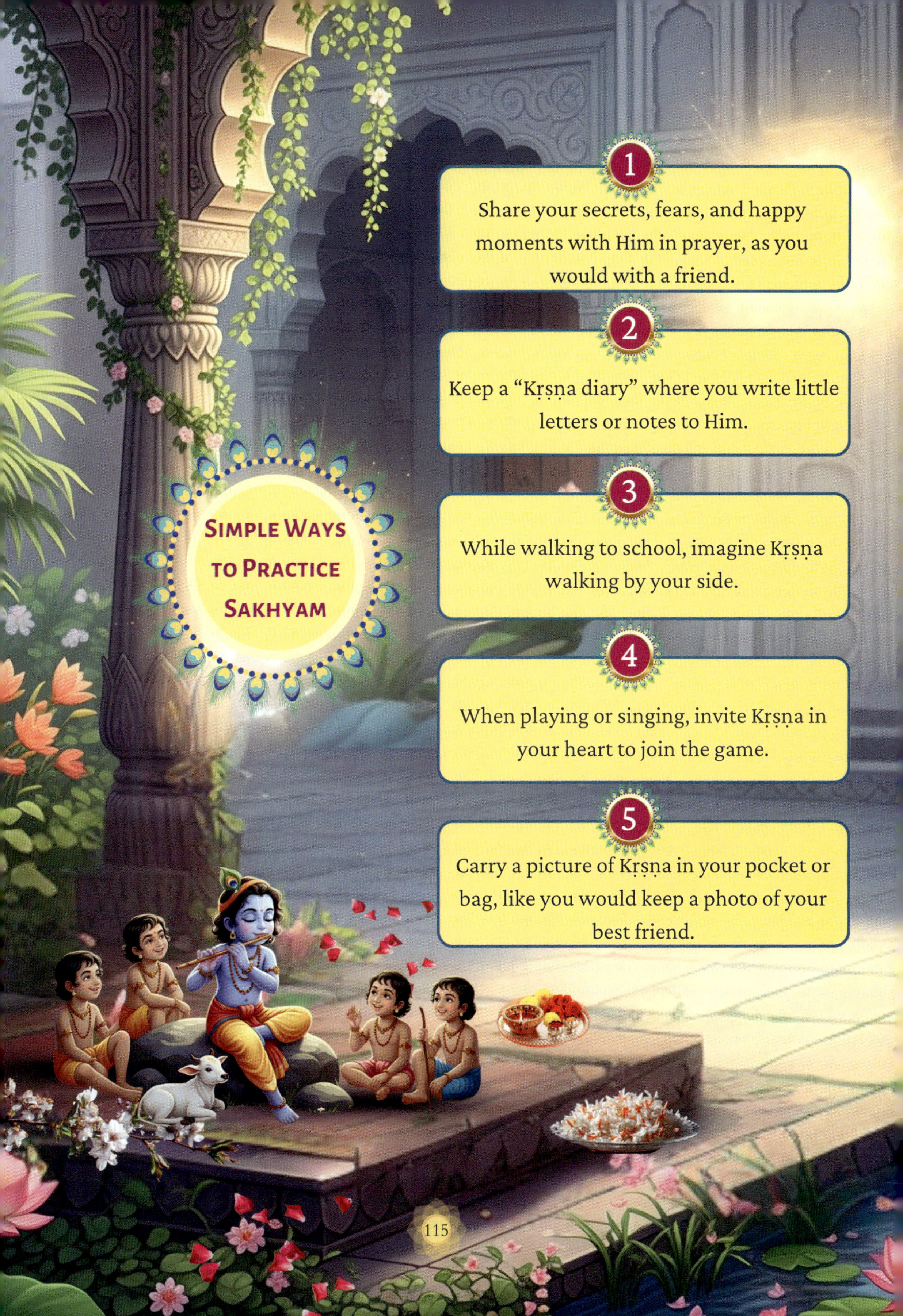


Simple Ways to Practice Sakhyam

1
Share your secrets, fears, and happy moments with Him in prayer, as you would with a friend.

2
Keep a "Kṛṣṇa diary" where you write little letters or notes to Him.

3
While walking to school, imagine Kṛṣṇa walking by your side.

4
When playing or singing, invite Kṛṣṇa in your heart to join the game.

5
Carry a picture of Kṛṣṇa in your pocket or bag, like you would keep a photo of your best friend.

# 9

# Ātma-Nivedanam

## Complete Surrender

*Everything we have belongs to Kṛṣṇa — and so do we!*

*Bhakti* is not just about offering something to the Lord but offering ourselves to Him. After all, we eternally belong to Him. When a devotee offers everything one has — wealth, power, skills, possessions, positions, and even their very self — that act of complete surrender is called *ātma-nivedanam*. It is the ultimate form of *bhakti*, the crown jewel that shines above all spiritual practices.

In fact, all the earlier processes of *bhakti* — hearing, chanting, remembering, serving, worshiping, or praying — naturally blossom into this final stage: full surrender. When we love someone completely, we don't hold anything back.

You may wonder: "But if I give everything to God, what about my own needs, wishes, or happiness?"

Imagine a small child resting in the arms of a loving parent. Does the child worry about food, safety, or protection? No — the child feels completely safe, trusting: "My parents will take care of me." That feeling of total trust and dependence is what *ātma-nivedanam* means.

In truth, we are already dependent on the Lord — whether we accept it or not! Everything we own comes from Him, and even we ourselves belong to Him. Surrender simply means accepting that eternal fact. And that was the final instruction of Lord Kṛṣṇa to Arjuna in the *Bhagavad-gītā*:

*sarva-dharmān parityajya mām ekaṁ śaraṇaṁ vraja*
*ahaṁ tvāṁ sarva-pāpebhyo mokṣayiṣyāmi mā śucaḥ*

"Give up all other duties and simply surrender to Me. I will protect you from all sins. Do not fear." (BG 18.66)

Surrender is not a weakness. It is the greatest strength. When we surrender to Kṛṣṇa, we no longer feel alone, scared, or burdened — because we trust that He is carrying us. Just like a sturdy boat carries a passenger across a river, Kṛṣṇa carries His surrendered devotee across the ocean of material life.

*Ātma-nivedanam* is the crown of *bhakti* — where love becomes whole, complete, and unbreakable. In such a mood a devotee dedicates everything one has and one is to the Lord.



"According to your nature, whatever you do—using your body, your words, your mind, your senses, or your intelligence—do it as an offering to Lord Nārāyaṇa, always thinking, 'I am doing this to please the Lord.'" (SB 11.2.36)

The following stories will show us shining examples of devotees who gave their hearts and lives fully to the Lord.

# 1. Bali Mahārāja – Surrendering All He Had

Bali Mahārāja was a powerful king of the demons, and the grandson of the great devotee Prahlāda Mahārāja. Because of the blessings of his guru and the brāhmaṇas, Bali became so strong that he conquered the heavenly planets, and Indra and the other devatās had to flee. Distressed, their mother Aditi prayed to Lord Viṣṇu for help.

The Lord answered her prayers in a very surprising way. He did not come as a fierce warrior but as a gentle brāhmaṇa boy, Vāmanadeva — short in size, but effulgent and glowing like the sun. Holding a staff and umbrella, Vāmana looked so charming that no one guessed He was the Supreme Lord Himself.

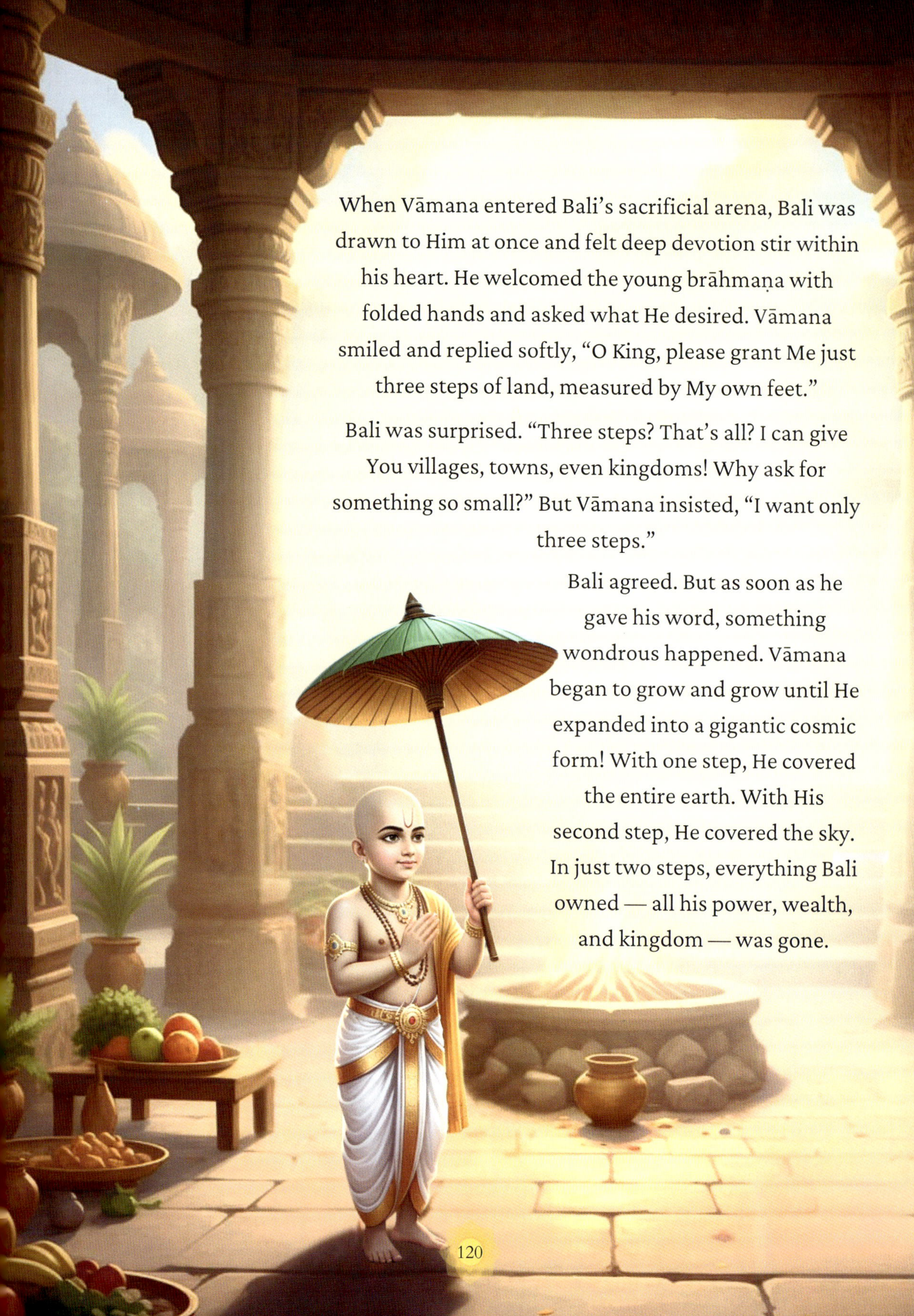

When Vāmana entered Bali's sacrificial arena, Bali was drawn to Him at once and felt deep devotion stir within his heart. He welcomed the young brāhmaṇa with folded hands and asked what He desired. Vāmana smiled and replied softly, "O King, please grant Me just three steps of land, measured by My own feet."

Bali was surprised. "Three steps? That's all? I can give You villages, towns, even kingdoms! Why ask for something so small?" But Vāmana insisted, "I want only three steps."

Bali agreed. But as soon as he gave his word, something wondrous happened. Vāmana began to grow and grow until He expanded into a gigantic cosmic form! With one step, He covered the entire earth. With His second step, He covered the sky. In just two steps, everything Bali owned — all his power, wealth, and kingdom — was gone.

Bali agreed. But as soon as he gave his word, something wondrous happened. Vāmana began to grow and grow until He expanded into a gigantic cosmic form! With one step, He covered the entire earth. With His second step, He covered the sky. In just two steps, everything Bali owned — all his power, wealth, and kingdom — was gone.

Then the Lord asked, "Bali, you promised Me three steps of land. Where shall I place My third step?"

The entire assembly was struck with wonder. Bali had nothing left. Bowing down humbly, he said with folded hands, "O Lord, I have lost everything. But I still have myself. Please place Your third step on my head."

Hearing these words, Vāmana was overjoyed. He placed His divine foot on Bali's head, blessing him with surrender, and granted him the kingdom of Sutala, a heavenly planet beneath the earth. But most wonderfully, the Lord Himself became Bali's doorkeeper, standing guard at Sutala forever to protect His devotee.

Bali Mahārāja lost all his worldly possessions, but by offering himself, he gained the Lord's eternal presence.

*When we give ourselves to the Lord, He gives Himself to us.*

## 2. Vibhīṣaṇa – Surrendering Against All Odds

Vibhīṣaṇa, the younger brother of the mighty demon king Rāvaṇa, was very different from the rest of his family. While Rāvaṇa and his followers were filled with pride and cruelty, Vibhīṣaṇa's heart was gentle and devoted to Lord Rāma.

When Rāvaṇa kidnapped Mother Sītā and brought her to Laṅkā, Vibhīṣaṇa repeatedly advised him: "Dear brother, Rāma is no ordinary man — He is the Supreme Lord. If you return Mother Sītā and seek His shelter, He will forgive you." But Rāvaṇa, blinded by arrogance, became furious. He insulted and rejected Vibhīṣaṇa's advice.

At that moment, Vibhīṣaṇa made a bold decision. He left behind his kingdom, wealth, and even his own brother, and chose to surrender to Lord Rāma. Taking only four loyal ministers with him, Vibhīṣaṇa crossed the ocean and arrived near Rāma's camp, calling out: "O Lord Rāma, I surrender myself at Your lotus feet!"

Some of Rāma's warriors were doubtful. "Can we trust him? He is Rāvaṇa's brother!" they argued. But Hanumān, who understood Vibhīṣaṇa's sincerity, spoke in his favor. Then Lord Rāma, with His compassionate heart, declared: "Whoever sincerely surrenders to Me, I will never reject him. I will always give him My protection."

Hearing these words, Rāma embraced Vibhīṣaṇa and accepted him as His devotee and friend. Later, Vibhīṣaṇa helped Rāma in the great battle against Rāvaṇa, and after Rāvaṇa's defeat, Rāma crowned him the king of Laṅkā.

The Lord is always ready to give shelter to those who surrender. We just need to make the choice —like Vibhīṣaṇa did.

Long ago, there was a great devotee named King Citraketu. By a curse from Mother Pārvatī, he had to take birth again as a demon named Vṛtrāsura. Though he looked fearsome on the outside, deep inside he remained a pure devotee of Lord Saṅkarṣaṇa. His heart always remembered the Lord.

As a demon, Vṛtrāsura fought the *devatas*. Seeing his gigantic body, the *devatas* attacked him with their weapons—but he swallowed them all! Terrified, they went to Lord Viṣṇu, who told them to ask Sage Dadhīci for his bones. From those bones they made a powerful thunderbolt, the Vajra, which Lord Viṣṇu Himself declared would kill Vṛtrāsura. Vṛtrāsura knew that his dear Lord had arranged everything— even his own death. Instead of complaining, he accepted it as the Lord's will.

When the battle began, Indra threw his club, but Vṛtrāsura caught it with ease and struck back. Airāvata, Indra's elephant, fell bleeding, but Indra revived him. Still, Indra hesitated to use the vajra. Seeing this, Vṛtrāsura encouraged him: "Don't be afraid! The thunderbolt given by the Lord cannot fail. Use it against me. If I die, I will be free from this demon's body and my mind will fly to the lotus feet of Lord Saṅkarṣaṇa. There I will serve Him and join the company of great devotees like Nārada Muni. Why should I want heaven, wealth, or even liberation? All I want is to serve the Lord and be with His devotees forever."

Even while fighting, Vṛtrāsura prayed: "O Lord, let my mind always think of You. Let my words glorify You. Let my hands serve You. I do not desire kingdoms, planets or powers. I only wish for the chance to serve You in the company of Your devotees." Hearing this, Indra was astonished. He said, "Though you appear as a demon, your mind is fixed on Lord Vāsudeva. You are a perfect devotee."

The battle raged on. Vṛtrāsura lost his arms, yet fought bravely, and finally swallowed Indra. He fixed his mind on the Lord and entered deep trance. Indra cut his way out of Vṛtrāsura's body and, after a long struggle, finally cut off Vṛtrāsura's head with the vajra. Vṛtrāsura was not in external consciousness, he soared upward, and entered the eternal abode of Lord Saṅkarṣaṇa.

True devotion means accepting
the Lord's plan with faith.

Rūpa and Sanātana were ministers in the government of Bengal under Nawab Hussain Shah. They were extremely wealthy, powerful, and respected. They had palaces, jewels, servants, and every kind of comfort. But deep in their hearts, they longed only for the service of Lord Caitanya Mahāprabhu.

When they heard about Caitanya Mahāprabhu spreading saṅkīrtana and drowning everyone in the nectar of bhakti, their hearts melted. They realized: "All this wealth and power is meaningless. Our only real treasure is the service of the Lord."

So, Rūpa Gosvāmī resigned from his post. He distributed his immense fortune — giving half to the *brāhmaṇas and Vaiṣṇavas*, a quarter to his relatives, and kept only a small portion for emergencies. Then he set out to join Mahāprabhu.

Sanātana Gosvāmī's path was harder. The Nawab did not want to let him go. He was even arrested and put in prison. But Sanātana was determined. He bribed the jailer with gold coins and escaped, walking barefoot through forests until he reached Lord Caitanya.

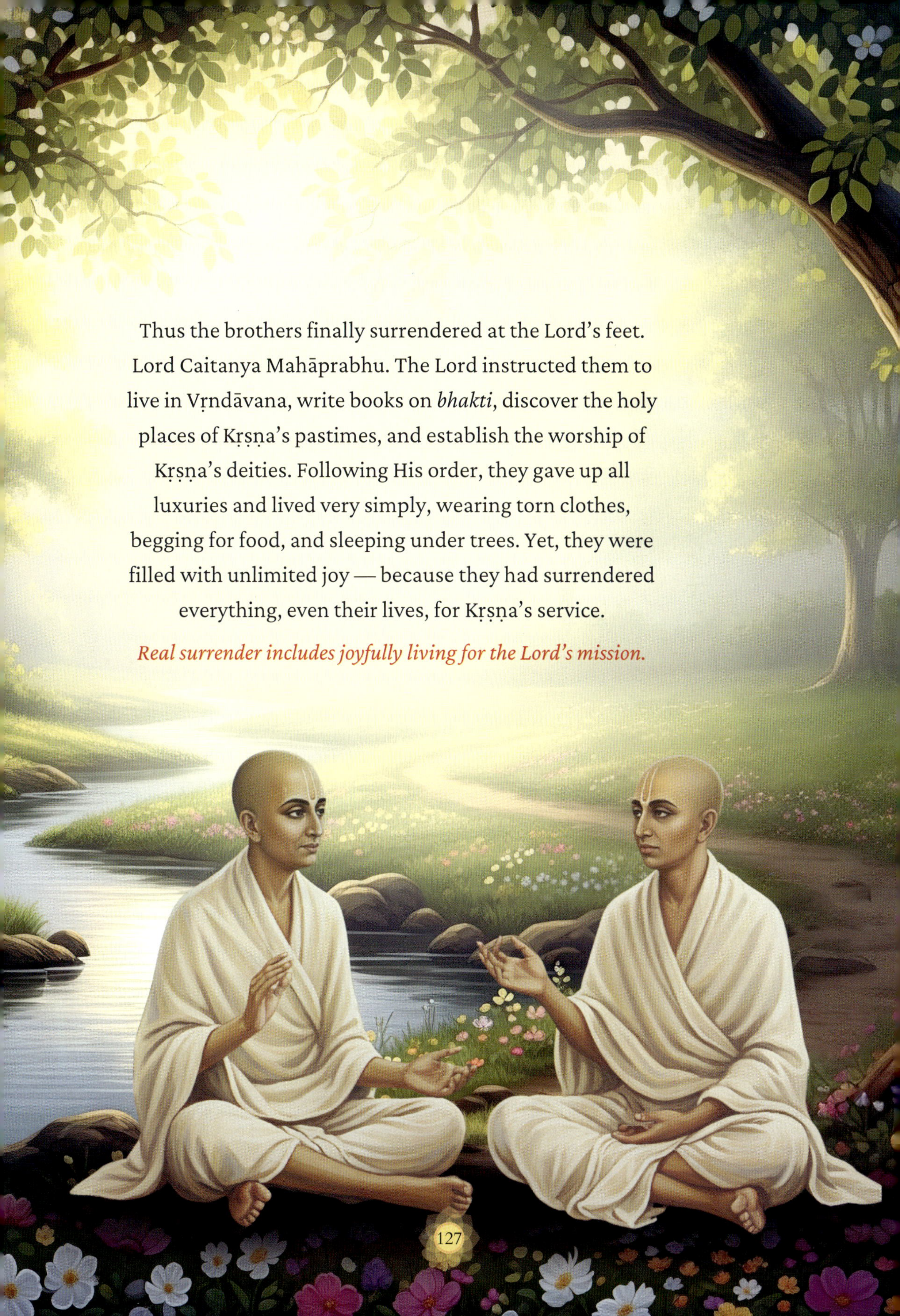

Thus the brothers finally surrendered at the Lord's feet. Lord Caitanya Mahāprabhu. The Lord instructed them to live in Vṛndāvana, write books on *bhakti*, discover the holy places of Kṛṣṇa's pastimes, and establish the worship of Kṛṣṇa's deities. Following His order, they gave up all luxuries and lived very simply, wearing torn clothes, begging for food, and sleeping under trees. Yet, they were filled with unlimited joy — because they had surrendered everything, even their lives, for Kṛṣṇa's service.

*Real surrender includes joyfully living for the Lord's mission.*

# Let's Surrender!

Surrender means trusting that the Lord always knows what is best for us. Just as Bali Mahārāja gave up everything for Lord Vāmana and Vṛtrāsura happily accepted the Lord's plan, we too can surrender our hearts. Surrender does not mean becoming weak—it means becoming strong by depending on Kṛṣṇa. When we surrender, we stop worrying about controlling everything and instead let the Lord guide our lives.

## Benefits of Surrender

| | | |
|---|---|---|
| 1 | **Fearlessness** | Surrendered devotees are never afraid, even in danger. |
| 2 | **Peace** | We stop struggling and feel light, because the Lord takes care of us. |
| 3 | **Happiness** | Material things can't give lasting joy, but surrendering to Kṛṣṇa brings deep happiness. |
| 4 | **Protection** | Kṛṣṇa promises, "I will protect you from all sinful reactions." |
| 5 | **Realization** | By surrendering, we realize we are Kṛṣṇa's eternal servants and friends. |

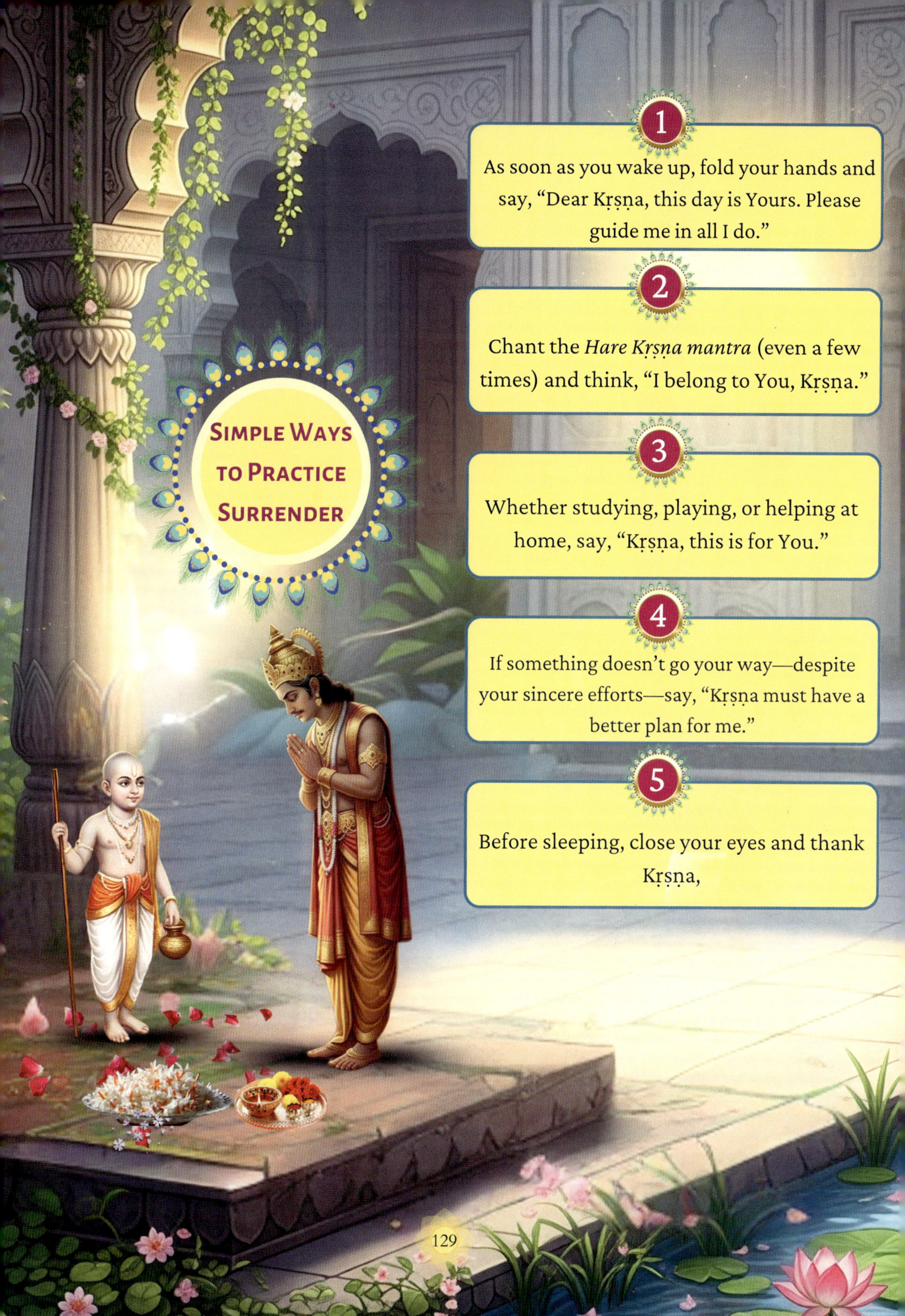

SIMPLE WAYS TO PRACTICE SURRENDER

1
As soon as you wake up, fold your hands and say, "Dear Kṛṣṇa, this day is Yours. Please guide me in all I do."

2
Chant the *Hare Kṛṣṇa mantra* (even a few times) and think, "I belong to You, Kṛṣṇa."

3
Whether studying, playing, or helping at home, say, "Kṛṣṇa, this is for You."

4
If something doesn't go your way—despite your sincere efforts—say, "Kṛṣṇa must have a better plan for me."

5
Before sleeping, close your eyes and thank Kṛṣṇa,

# EPILOGUE

Dear children, hope you have enjoyed and been inspired by learning about the nine ways of *bhakti* and the 50 stories of great devotees, each of whom practiced one or more of these beautiful paths — from *śravaṇam* (hearing) to *ātma-nivedanam* (surrender). Each of the nine processes of *bhakti* is so powerful that even by sincerely following just one of them, a devotee can achieve perfection in devotion.

When a devotee steadily performs one way of bhakti as the main practice, with the others supporting it, it is called *eka-aṅga bhakti*. When many ways are practiced together according to one's inspiration, it is called *aneka-aṅga bhakti*.

Both lead to the same goal — awakening pure love and heartfelt emotions for Lord Kṛṣṇa.

A very special devotee named Mahārāja Ambarīṣa showed how one can practice multiple or all ways of bhakti together by engaging every limb of the body in Kṛṣṇa's service:

# Bhakti of Mahārāja Ambarīṣa

*sa vai manaḥ kṛṣṇa-padāravindayor*

Mind in meditating on Kṛṣṇa's lotus feet

*vacāṁsi vaikuṇṭha-guṇānuvarṇane*

Words in glorifying Kṛṣṇa's qualities.

*karau harer mandira-mārjanādiṣu*

Hands in cleaning Lord Hari's temple.

*śrutiṁ cakārācyuta-sat-kathodaye*

Ears in hearing narrations about Kṛṣṇa

*mukunda-liṅgālaya-darśane dṛśau*

Eyes in seeing the deities of Mukunda.

*tad-bhṛtya-gātra-sparśe 'ṅga-saṅgamam*

Sense of touch in touching devotees' bodies

*ghrāṇaṁ ca tat-pāda-saroja-saurabhe śrīmat-tulasyā*

Sense of smell in relishing the fragrance of tulasi at the Lord's feet

*rasanāṁ tad-arpite*

Tongue in tasting the Lord's prasāda

*pādau hareḥ kṣetra-padānusarpaṇe*

Legs in walking to holy places and temples

*śiro hṛṣīkeśa-padābhivandane*

Head in bowing to Lord Hṛṣīkeśa's feet

*kāmaṁ ca dāsye na tu kāma-kāmyayā*

Desires in Lord's service, not enjoyment

*yathottamaśloka-janāśrayā ratiḥ*

He did all this to develop attachment for the Lord as possessed by great devotees

There is a beautiful verse that highlights one shining example for each of the nine ways of devotion. As we conclude this book, let us meditate on this *śloka:*

*śrī-viṣṇoḥ śravaṇe parīkṣid abhavad vaiyāsakiḥ kīrtane*
*prahlādaḥ smaraṇe tad-aṅghri-bhajane lakṣmīḥ pṛthuḥ pūjane*
*akrūras tv abhivandane kapi-patir dāsye 'tha sakhye 'rjunaḥ*
*sarvasvātma-nivedane balir abhūt kṛṣṇāptir eṣāṁ param*

"King Parīkṣit attained perfection by hearing, Śukadeva Gosvāmī by chanting, Prahlāda by remembering, Lakṣmī Devī by serving the Lord's feet, King Pṛthu by worship, Akrūra by offering prayers, Hanumān by serving, Arjuna by friendship, and Bali Mahārāja by surrendering everything." (*Rūpa Gosvāmī's Padyāvalī 53*)

# ACKNOWLEDGEMENTS

Words are not sufficient to express my heartfelt gratitude to Śrīla Prabhupāda, who gifted the world the priceless treasure of scriptures with his lucid yet profound explanations. I cannot imagine comprehending these sacred texts without his enlightening translations and purports.

I am eternally indebted to my beloved spiritual master, His Holiness Radhanath Swami Maharaja, whose affectionate blessings and encouragement have inspired me to study and share the message of the scriptures. I am deeply grateful to him emphasizing the importance of *Vaiṣṇava* humility and the proper mood of approaching scriptures through his teachings and dealings.

I sincerely thank Gauranga Prabhu for giving me the opportunity to serve the scriptures and those seeking to understand them. Special thanks to my dear friend Madhav Gopal Prabhu, who reviewed my manuscript and checked for the accuracy of the content.

I am very grateful to Durga Prasad Prabhu, who spent countless hours creating the illustrations for this book. Without his selfless effort and patience, this book would not have taken its present form. I also humbly thank Srilakshmi Mataji for wonderfully designing the book with dedication, and the young brothers Tanay and Parth, for their help in proofreading. My humble prayers and best wishes are with all these devotees in their continued journey in Kṛṣṇa consciousness. My heartfelt gratitude to the entire Tulsi Books team for making this publication possible.

Lastly, I express my sincere thanks to all the wonderful children who attended my courses. Their innocent yet intelligent questions and lively interactions gave me valuable insights into their needs and perspectives, helping me write for them more effectively. I also extend my deep respect to their parents and teachers, who have nurtured them so beautifully.

It is my earnest prayer that this work serves as a source of inspiration for all who wish to deepen their devotion to Lord Śrī Kṛṣṇa.

# Books by the Author

## Study Guides

 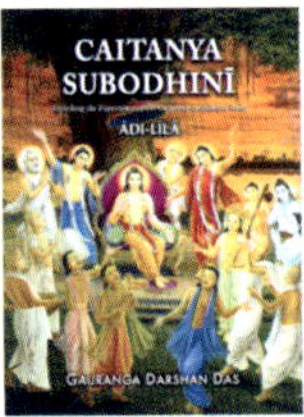   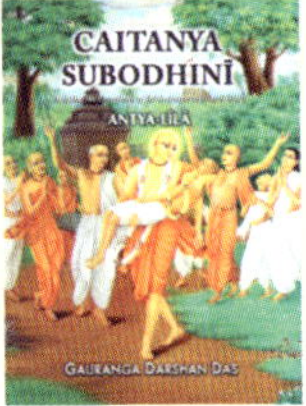 

   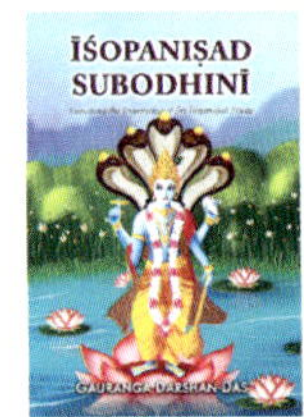  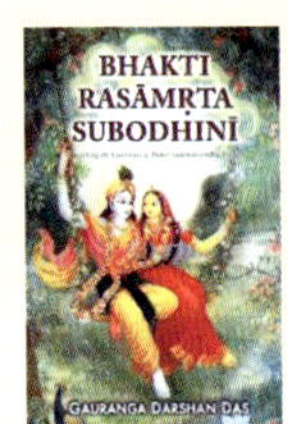

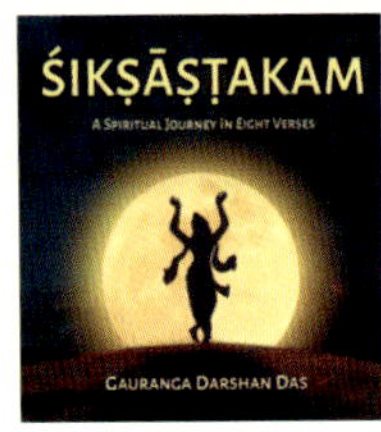  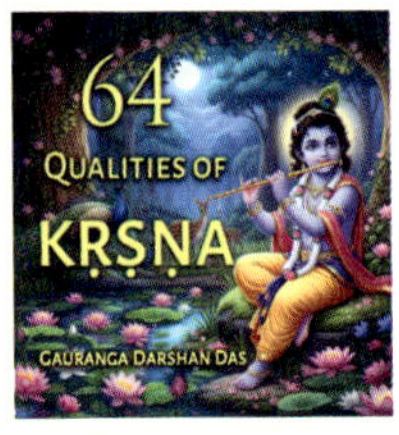

## Self Enrichment

 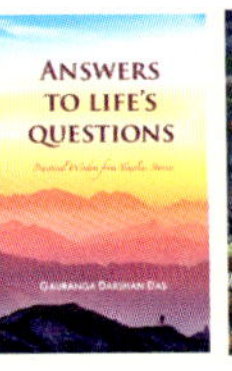   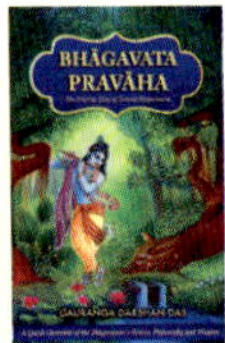   

# ILLUSTRATED CHILDREN BOOKS

## SHLOKA BOOKS

## CHILDREN WORKBOOKS

## TRANSLATED WORKS

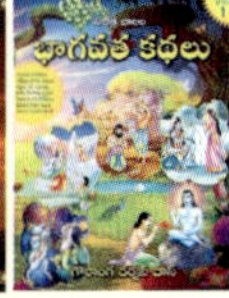

**TELUGU**

**HINDI**

**GUJARATI**

**MARATHI**

# About the Author

Gauranga Darshan Das, a disciple of His Holiness Radhanath Swami, is a spiritual educator and an author of over 46 books. He holds a Master's in Systems Science and Automation from the prestigious Indian Institute of Science (IISc), Bangalore, India. His outstanding contributions have earned him accolades such as the "Visionary Leader: Spirituality" award from Brand Vision Inc. and the "Spiritual Scientist" award from Andhra University.

Before embracing monkhood in 2009, Gauranga Darshan Das had a brief yet impactful corporate career spanning two years. During this time, he conducted research at renowned organizations like TCS Innovation Labs, authored over 10 technical papers, and filed a provisional patent for his research.

Currently, he serves as the Dean of Bhaktivedanta Vidyapitha at ISKCON Govardhan Ecovillage (GEV), where he leads both residential and online spiritual education programs. With his ability to present timeless wisdom in a lucid and contemporary style, he connects with diverse audiences, including children, teens, professionals and educators. His speaking and teaching engagements span India, Australia, the United States, the United Kingdom, New Zealand, Singapore, and other countries. He has addressed audiences in spiritual organizations, schools, colleges, and corporate sectors, and on prominent platforms like TEDx, ISRO, DRDO, and Hindustan Times. To date, he has delivered over 8500 hours of lectures and conducted more than 50 online courses, available at www.vidyapitha.in.

As an accomplished author, Gauranga Darshan Das has written over 46 books. His works include study guides (such as the Subodhini series), storybooks, self-enrichment titles (From Chaos to Calm, Dhruva, Disapproved but not Disowned, and more), and children's literature (Mindful Me!, Bhagavatam Tales, and Gita Wisdom Tales series). He also runs a monthly e-zine, Bhagavata Pradipika, and contributes thought-provoking articles to Back to Godhead magazines in India and internationally. Know more about his inspiring work at www.gaurangadarshan.com.